HOSPITALLERS

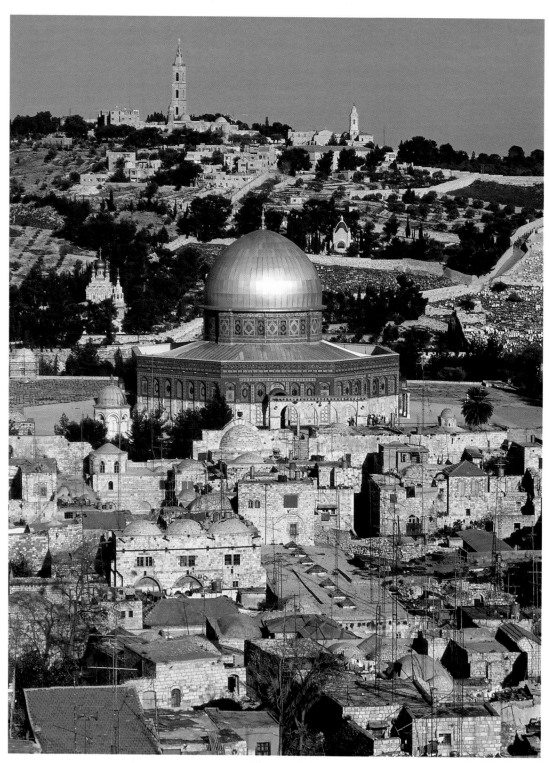

FRONTISPIECE. The Dome of the Rock, Jerusalem

HOSPITALLERS

*The History of the
Order of St John*

JONATHAN RILEY-SMITH

THE HAMBLEDON PRESS
London and Rio Grande

Published by the Hambledon Press 1999

102 Gloucester Avenue, London NW1 8HX (UK)
PO Box 162, Rio Grande, Ohio 45674 (USA)

ISBN 1 85285 196 1 (cased)
ISBN 1 85285 197 X (paper)

A description of this book is available from
the British Library and from the Library of Congress

Typeset in Baskerville and Gill Sans and originated
by Carnegie Publishing, Chatsworth Rd, Lancaster
Printed on acid-free paper and bound in Great Britain
by The Bath Press

Picture acknowledgements

Museum of the Order of St John, St John's Gate, London EC1M 4DA
(photography, Rod Tidnam), pp. 7, 8, 11, 13, 15, 16 below, 20, 22, 25, 26, 28,
29, 30, 38, 41, 44, 45 below, 48, 50, 54, 56, 57, 59 below, 64, 66, 67, 69, 72, 73,
75, 76, 77, 78 middle right, 79 left, 80 below, 81, 82, 83, 84 top, 85, 86, 87, 88,
89, 93 (not bottom right), 96, 97, 98, 99, 100, 101, 104 top, 106, 107, 110, 111,
112, 113, 114, 115, 116, 117, 118, 119, 120, 121, 122, 123, 125, 126, 130, 131, 132,
133, 134, 135, 136, 137, 138, 140, 141, 142, 143, 144; PR Department, St John
Ambulance, pp. 146, 147, 148, 149, 150, 151.

Azzopardi, *The Order's Early Legacy in Malta* (Malta, 1989), p. 19; Bibliothèque
Nationale, Paris, MS Lat. 6067, fol. 83v, p. 68; fol. 3v, p. 70; fol. 120v, p. 71;
fol. 37v, p. 90; fol. 33v, p. 91; fol. 9v, p. 92; fol. 79, p. 103; fol. 79v, p. 105;
Bibliothèque Royale, Brussels, Cabinet des Manuscrits, no. 11.142, fol. 1, p. 55;
British Library, p. 5, MS Royal 15.E.2, fol. 165; p. 24, MS Royal 20.C.VII,
fol. 48, p. 52; MS Add. 18143, fol. 3v, p. 104 below; Henry Brownrigg, p. 78
below left; Instituto de Estudios Sijenenses, Sijena, p. 63; Ghent University,
p. 80; A. F. Kersting, pp. 27, 84 below, 93 bottom right, 94, 102; Kunst-
historisches Museum, Vienna, p. 58; Studio M. Martin, Milhaud, p. 78 top; M.
Miguet, p. 32; Musée Lorraine, Nancy (photo P. Mignot), p. 6; James Nash, p.
45 above, p. 46 above, p. 61; National Museum of Fine Arts, Valletta, Malta,
pp. 59 top, 108, 109; National Portrait Gallery, p. 129; Alistair Duncan, p. ii;
Pierpont Morgan Library, New York, MS Glazier 55, fol. 125v, p. 65; MS
Glazier 55, fol. 140v, p. 95; Elizabeth de Ranitz-Labouchere, pp 37, 42;
Jonathan Riley-Smith, pp. 16 top, 17, 35, 43, 46 below, 48 below left; Scala
Photo Library, p. 62; Sotheby's, p. 79 right; Swanston Publishing, p. 4;
Templecombe Church, p. 53; Wellcome Institute Library, MS Western 49, fol.
38, p. 23; Pamela Willis, pp. 82 top right and below, 84 top, 85 top.

Contents

Foreword

by HRH the Duke of Gloucester

The Hospitallers were a military and religious order founded in Jerusalem before the First Crusade in 1099, dedicated to caring for the sick and to the defence of Christendom. Their descendants today are the recognised orders of St John – the Sovereign Military Order of Malta, the Johanniter orders in Germany, in the Netherlands and Sweden, and their associate bodies in Finland, Switzerland, Hungary and France, together with, in Britain, the Most Venerable Order of the Hospital of St John of Jerusalem, of which I have the honour, under the order's Sovereign Head, the Queen, to be the Grand Prior. Together we are celebrating 900 years of tradition, struggle and hard work, most skilfully traced in this book by Professor Riley-Smith.

The order in Britain has known hard times. Wat Tyler burned down its priory at Clerkenwell; Henry VIII dissolved it. But Queen Victoria gave the modern British order a royal charter in 1888, recognising the resurgence of the Hospitaller tradition which had brought about the foundation of the St John Ambulance Association and Brigade (all volunteers) in a Britain which badly needed organized emergency medical care. It also brought the foundation of the St John Ophthalmic Hospital in East Jerusalem, a much-loved institution which flourishes today, and has recently expanded to include a clinic in Gaza. With priories in Scotland, Wales, South Africa, New Zealand, Canada, Australia and the United States, and with branches in thirty former Commonwealth countries, caring for the sick and the poor is our business today as it was for the Hospitallers in 1099.

I am proud to be so closely associated with St John and I welcome Jonathan Riley-Smith's book. The volunteer tradition is under threat today, but the Hospitallers, as Professor Riley-Smith so clearly shows, know all about overcoming pressures.

Introduction

The order of St John of Jerusalem came into existence as a pilgrim hospital in a Jerusalem which was still under Muslim control. Twenty years later, in 1099, the First Crusade took the city and the two centuries of Christian government in the Levant that followed provided the environment in which the Hospital grew into a military order, without abandoning its responsibilities for the care of the sick poor. From the late twelfth century until well into the nineteenth its military functions were of prime importance to it and with them came great wealth, a degree of political power and, as the ruler of island principalities, first Rhodes from 1309 to 1523 and then Malta from 1530 to 1798, recognition as a sovereign entity. But from the 1840s, in a world which had turned its back on crusading, it reverted to its original function of caring only for the sick, although it still retains, in its ethos and customs, some vestiges of its long military career. Meanwhile Protestant confraternities, claiming descent from it and a share in its traditions, emerged in northern Europe and were recognized in their respective countries as orders of St John. The St John family crosses confessional divides, uniting all those associated with it in their service to the sick and the poor.

There are several other famous international charities, but none are quite like St John. It is the oldest specialized Christian charitable movement, originating in an order of the church which has always been unusual in that it is run not by ordained priests but by lay brothers. Other medieval orders – the Benedictine and Franciscan, for instance – have seen non-Catholic branches emerge, but nowhere else are relations as close as they have become between the five recognized orders of St John, which provide a model of practical ecumenism. In England and in Germany, moreover, the volunteers are so many and the wings to which they belong have been in existence for so long that they have generated their own grass-roots versions of the St John ethos, with generation after generation of the same families involved. It is, for example, possible to see in England parallels between St John Ambulance and the Salvation Army. St John, always adapting to meet new demands, has the potential to expand in a world which desperately needs the services it offers.

The Crusades

Pilgrimages to Jerusalem

Pilgrimage to sites regarded as holy is as old as mankind. Christian pilgrims were certainly on the roads within a century of Christ's crucifixion, although the first surviving account of a journey to Jerusalem dates from the year 333. Then came the rise of Islam in the seventh century and its conquest of the Levant and North Africa. There were fewer western visitors to Jerusalem after the city fell to the Muslims in 638. This may have been due more to the uncertainties of the journey than any difficulties created by the authorities in Palestine.

Pilgrimage from the west began to pick up again in the tenth century. The flow of pilgrims seems to have been on the way to becoming a flood around the year 1000, although it was then briefly interrupted by persecutions, resuming again around 1020. The increased traffic probably reflected anxiety that the Last Days were near as the millennium (the year 1000 and then the year 1033) approached, for it was to be in Jerusalem that the final acts in this dimension – the appearance of Anti-Christ, the return of the Saviour, the earliest splitting of tombs and reassembling of bones and dust in the General Resurrection – would take place. Contemporary piety anyway encouraged a feverish obsession with pilgrimage, which was for most people the natural way of showing religious feeling and sorrow for sin.

Their state of mind on departure, and the way monks resorted to age-old techniques to exploit it, are illustrated by events at the start of the fourth pilgrimage to Jerusalem of Count Fulk III of Anjou in the late 1030s. Fulk, who had ruled Anjou for fifty-three years with energetic violence, combined ferocity with exceptional piety, so that during his life acts of bestial cruelty regularly alternated with extravagant expressions of devotion. Now an old man, he spent the first night of the journey at the abbey of St-Maur-sur-Loire. His party was honourably received and given a magnificent meal, during which one of the monks read from the Life of St Maur. After the meal the bishop of Angers entertained the company with stories about the saint and so fired Fulk that he was persuaded then and there to finance the rebuilding of the abbey church. Once in Jerusalem he stripped himself naked and had himself led to the Holy Sepulchre, the most sacred site of all because it was believed to be the tomb from which Christ had risen, by a halter looped round his neck, while a servant scourged his back and he called on Christ to accept his penance.

Europe and the Near East showing religious divisions.

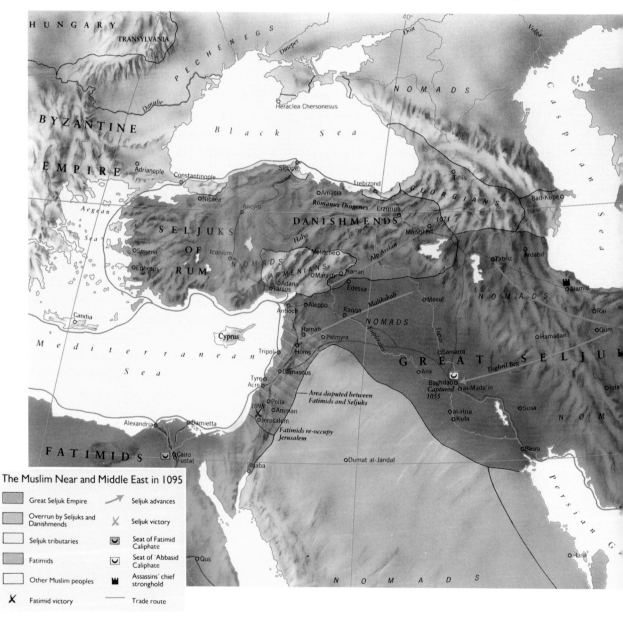

The Muslim Near and Middle East in 1095

Great Seljuk Empire	→	Seljuk advances
Overrun by Seljuks and Danishmends	✗	Seljuk victory
Seljuk tributaries	⊍	Seat of Fatimid Caliphate
Fatimids	⊍	Seat of 'Abbasid Caliphate
Other Muslim peoples	♜	Assassins' chief stronghold
✗ Fatimid victory	—	Trade route

✠ 4 ✠

A twelfth-century pilgrim with palm fronds, church of St-Nicholas, Tavant, France. Before starting for home the first crusaders would throw their arms and armour away, travelling as simple pilgrims and carrying palm fronds, the mark of a successful pilgrimage to Jerusalem. Several palms were deposited, almost as relics, in western churches.

By the mid 1020s there is evidence for many pilgrims to Jerusalem being on the move and other major waves seem to have surged east in the 1030s, the 1050s and the 1060s. In the 1070s passage across Asia Minor, now being overrun by nomadic Turks, must have become much more difficult, but the traffic does not seem to have lessened – perhaps more people were travelling by sea – and it certainly increased again in the 1080s and early 1090s, when many men and women were making the journey. It could be made surprisingly quickly. In 1026 Count William Taillefer of Angoulême left home on 1 October and reached Jerusalem just over five months later, in the first week of the following March. But there were discomforts and worse. In 1022 Gerald of Thouars, the abbot of St-Florent-lès-Saumur, was taken prisoner and, it was believed, martyred by Muslims before he reached Jerusalem. Four years later Richard of St-Vanne was stoned when he said mass openly in Islamic territory – the Muslims tolerated Christian worship provided it was not done publicly – and the atmosphere in Jerusalem seems to have been tense: stones were thrown into the Sepulchre compound during Holy Week and the pilgrims were worried by the number of armed men in the streets. In 1040 Ulrich of Breisgau, whose pilgrimage was eccentric – he took with him one servant and one horse, which he never rode until he had recited the whole psalter – was stoned by a hostile crowd near the River Jordan. In 1055 the authorities expelled the Christians from the Sepulchre compound and closed the pilgrim roads for a time, and in 1065 a large German pilgrimage was ambushed on the Palestinian plain and severely mauled; it was reported later that two-thirds of the party did not return to the west.

Pilgrimage

Pilgrims to Jerusalem were, broadly speaking, of three types:

✠ Those, like Fulk of Anjou, who were performing a penance imposed on them by a confessor. By the thirteenth century this category had been defined and further subdivided into three, depending on the nature of the sin and the status of the confessor.

✠ Those undertaking what was called a *peregrinatio religiosa* (a devotional pilgrimage). There was a penitential element in their journeys as well, but the pilgrimages were not enjoined by a confessor, being undertaken voluntarily, perhaps as a result of a vow.

✠ Those who were going to Jerusalem to live there until they died; the special position of the city in the geography of providence meant that it was a place in which devout Christians wanted to be buried.

Pilgrim Routes to Jerusalem

The first stage was to Constantinople. There were three possible ways to get there. All were used in the late 1090s by the armies of the First Crusade.

✠ Pilgrims would travel down through Italy to Bari, where they would take a boat across the Adriatic and then follow the old imperial road, the Via Egnatia, to Constantinople. This route was popular throughout the eleventh century.

✠ The conversion of Hungary had made the land passage through central Europe, the so-called 'Bavarian Road', much more secure. This passed through southern Germany and Hungary.

✠ A third route went south through Dalmatia to Durazzo and then joined the Via Egnatia. From Constantinople everyone seems to have taken the old imperial highway to the east which ran to Antioch, from where the pilgrims travelled south down the Syrian and Palestinian coasts. That final stretch – by way of Latakia, Tripoli, Caesarea and Ramle to Jerusalem – was considered to be a dangerous one.

The First Crusade

The problems pilgrims to Jerusalem faced in the eleventh century were compounded by instability in the Islamic world. Two rival caliphates, in Cairo and Baghdad, had embarked on a struggle

A crusader and his wife from the cloister of the priory of Belval in Lorraine. Is she saying goodbye or welcoming him home? Note that the crusader is dressed as a pilgrim, but with a cloth cross on his chest.

OPPOSITE AND OVERLEAF. The church of the Holy Sepulchre. It was only in the 1130s that the western settlers in Jerusalem conceived of the stupendous architectural plan of relating the sites of Christ's death and Resurrection to one another under one roof. Previously they had been separate shrines on two sides of a courtyard. The result was the greatest shrine church ever built. No cost was spared on its ornamentation.

✠ 7 ✠

for Palestine and Syria, which lay between them. Jerusalem was to change hands in 1071 and again in 1098, when the first crusaders were already in northern Syria. Cairo was the centre of a proselytizing Shi'ism and pockets of Shi'ites throughout the Islamic world challenged the hegemony of the Sunni 'Abbasid caliphate in Baghdad, which from 1055 was under the control of Turkish sultans, originating from among nomadic Turkoman peoples, who had lived on the borders of the steppe east of the Aral Sea. Strictly Sunni and hostile to Shi'ite Cairo, they had swept west, establishing a sultanate which ruled Iran, Iraq and part of Syria. Parties of Turkish nomads were also foraying into the territories of the Byzantine empire, the Greek Christian successor state of the eastern Roman empire centred on Constantinople. The destruction of a Byzantine army in the battle of Manzikert (26 August 1071) helped to open the empire to the nomads, who were anyway being employed by rebellious Greek generals in a period of political instability. Asia Minor quickly passed out of Byzantine control and it was this that led to appeals to the west for assistance.

Pope Urban II's response in 1095 was to preach the First Crusade during a year-long tour of France, beginning in the autumn of 1095. This opened a period of European history which was to last for seven centuries until Malta, the last order state under an active military order, succumbed to Napoleon in 1798. Crusading was not confined to the eastern Mediterranean region but came to be waged in Spain and Portugal, the Baltic litoral, eastern Europe, North Africa and the interior of western Europe. Its opponents came to be not only Muslims, but also Mongols, pagan Balts, Orthodox Greeks and Russians, heretics of various kinds and opponents of the papacy who were believed to be threatening the interests of the church. The popes, who proclaimed crusades as Christ's vicars and authorized the granting of crusade privileges, came to think strategically in transcontinental and intercontinental terms. They would decide where to commit resources, arousing fierce criticism from those theatres which they decided to ignore.

The First Crusade was a violent and brutal episode during which the crusaders cut a swathe of suffering through Europe and western Asia, even if perceptions in the west were influenced more by accounts of the trials undergone by the crusaders themselves; ordeals which, it is fairly clear, they had expected. The first parties, made up largely of poor people but under noble command, were already on the move in the spring of 1096, earlier than the pope had wished and before they could enjoy the benefits of that year's harvest. Most of them got no further than the Balkans, but before leaving the west many of them took part in a ferocious persecution of Jews, particularly in the Rhineland, but also in France, Bavaria and Bohemia, in the course of which the important Jewish community at Mainz was almost wiped out. Two of the early armies reached Constantinople relatively intact, but once they had crossed the Bosphorus they were cut to pieces by the Turks. They were followed from mid August onwards by contingents with more effective military components, although their progress was also impeded by the hordes of poor pilgrims who attached themselves to them. After long and sometimes dangerous marches across Europe, the crusaders arrived outside Constantinople in late 1096 and early 1097. They thought they were going to campaign under the command of the Byzantine Emperor Alexius, but they now had to face the realities of Byzantine politics, for the Greeks felt threatened by forces which were much larger than they had expected and used every means at their disposal, from blandishment to ill-treatment, to persuade each contingent to cross the Bosphorus into Asia independently as soon as possible after its arrival. The various elements of the crusade only came together before the walls of Nicaea, the first major city in Turkish hands, which surrendered to the Greeks on 19 June 1097.

A week later, realizing that they were not going to get the leadership and assistance from the Byzantine emperor they had expected, the crusaders struck out on their own across Asia Minor, accompanied by a token force of Greek soldiers and by guides. In late October, after an exhausting and traumatic march punctuated by victories over the Turks at Dorylaeum and Eregli, they reached Antioch, a city which, although a shadow of its former self, still controlled the easiest passes from Asia Minor into Syria. They invested it for seven and a half months, beating off two Muslim armies of relief. It fell to them on 3 June 1098, but almost at once they found themselves besieged in their turn by a new Muslim army, which would have caught them outside the walls had it not been held up for three weeks in a fruitless attempt to storm the town of Edessa, 160 miles to the north east and already in crusader hands. On the night of 10 June morale was so low and panic levels so high in the western army that its leaders had to seal the gates and patrol the walls to prevent a mass break-out, but this was followed by reports from visionaries of Christ appearing and promising victory and by the discovery of what was said to be the lance which had pierced His side when He was on the cross. It was generally believed that the whereabouts of this relic had been revealed to a Provençal servant called Peter Bartholomew by the Apostle Andrew himself. Their morale restored, the crusaders sortied out of the city on 28 June and in a victory attributed by some of them to the appearance on their left flank of a heavenly army

Crusade

A crusade was a war waged on Christ's behalf in defence of Christendom against external or internal injury. Each crusader vowed publicly to take part as an act of individual penance; in return he was granted an indulgence and enjoyed certain temporal privileges, the purpose of which was to make his task easier. Crusading bred two mutations: military orders, the members of which were not crusaders, being permanently as opposed to temporarily engaged in the defence of Christendom, sometimes operating out of little theocracies, their order states; and crusade leagues, which were alliances of certain front-line powers, the forces of which were granted crusade privileges.

Indulgence

The indulgence, the greatest privilege granted to crusaders, was at first an authoritative declaration by the pope that the penance (or voluntary self-punishment) which a crusader was undertaking was so severe that it would be 'satisfactory', in the sense that it would compensate for the debt owed by him or her to God for sin. By the end of the twelfth century the indulgence had become a privilege, granted by the pope on God's behalf, according to which God mercifully guaranteed to remit the punishment, in this world or the next, for sins previously committed, irrespective of whether the penance was satisfactory or not. The developed indulgence answered increasing anxieties as to whether any self-imposed punishment could ever be satisfactory in God's eyes.

Seal of indulgence for a donation to the order's castle at Bodrum.
Granted to John and Margaret Saville, early fourteenth century.

of angels, saints and the ghosts of their dead companions, routed the Muslims. Although the next move was not to be made for five months, this was the turning point of the campaign.

It was the poor who forced the leaders, who could not agree on the next step, to take the road again between 13 January and early February 1099. The crusaders seem to have planned the occupation of some of the major fortresses which lay in their path and could have cut their lifeline back to Antioch if held by the enemy, but after besieging 'Arqah in Lebanon in vain for three months they resolved to ignore the strongpoints and hurry down the coast while the countryside was still in a state to feed them – it was harvest time – and before the Egyptians could raise an army to intercept them. They reached Jerusalem on 7 June and the city fell to assault on 15 July. On 12 August a large Egyptian counter-invasion was thrown back near Ascalon. Of the army of 70,000 men and women, including 7000 knights, which had mustered at Nicaea two years before, only 12,000, of whom 1200 to 1300 were knights, besieged Jerusalem. Many crusaders had settled in Edessa and around Antioch and many others had deserted, but new arrivals had been joining the army all the time. It is likely that out of every four crusaders who had left Europe in 1096 only one survived three years later.

The survivors, however, thought of their companions as martyrs in a holy cause. Jerusalem was now in Christian hands and was to remain so until the Muslim ruler Saladin took it in 1187. For nearly ninety years it became the pilgrimage destination par excellence for Catholics from the west. Twice a year the fleets would arrive, bringing those who would not risk the perilous journey overland, and they would join many others – eastern Christians, Muslims and Jews – who had also come to to venerate the holy places.

The Latin East

In August 1099, in the immediate aftermath of the First Crusade, the Christian hold on the newly conquered territories was precarious. Those crusaders who had decided to remain in Palestine occupied only Jerusalem itself and a corridor of land stretching to Jaffa on the coast. Three hundred miles to the north there were islands of crusader government in Syria and northern Mesopotamia, but all these enclaves were under threat. Jerusalem

The Holy Sepulchre, Jerusalem

When the crusaders took Jerusalem in 1099 a compound enclosed several separate shrines, the most venerated of which was Christ's tomb, or what remained of it, detached in the fourth century by the Emperor Constantine's engineers from the rest of the quarry wall out of which it had been hollowed and encased in a small free-standing chapel which stood under a rotunda built in the mid eleventh century. Nearby was the site of the Crucifixion, the chapel of Calvary on top of the rock column to which the hill of Golgotha had been reduced, and, somewhat apart, the ruins of Constantine's basilica, built over the spot where his mother had reputedly discovered the wood of the True Cross in 320. In the 1140s, with Jerusalem under Latin rule, the locations of Christ's death and resurrection were physically related to each other for the first time under a single roof in one enormous, sumptuously decorated building, on of the most ambitious architectural ventures ever.

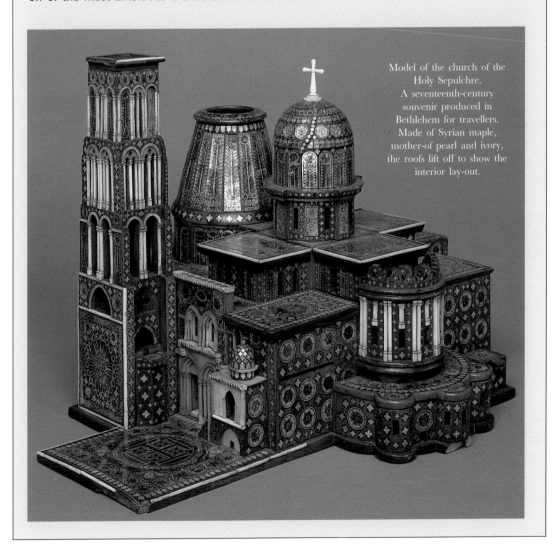

Model of the church of the Holy Sepulchre. A seventeenth-century souvenir produced in Bethlehem for travellers. Made of Syrian maple, mother-of pearl and ivory, the roofs lift off to show the interior lay-out.

was awkwardly placed geographically, had never had much economic importance and could not be held in isolation. Control had to be established over the region around it and there had to be a relatively secure line of communications back to Antioch and beyond. The ports were progressively reduced in a strategy which dominated the next twenty-five years and by 1124 the Christians

Forms of Islam

Whereas for Sunni Muslims (the majority) religious authority lies in the consensus of the community reflecting the holy law (the sharia), which has been shaped by the sunna, a body of orally transmitted traditions relating to the words and deeds of the Prophet and his companions, Shi'ites believe that supreme religious authority was held by Ali, the Prophet's son-in-law, and then by the imams who were his spiritual successors. One group of Shi'ites held that after the disappearance of the twelfth imam, in 878, spiritual authority was in abeyance until he returned; another group, the Isma'ilis, held that the Fatimid dynasty, which had established a Shi'ite caliphate in Cairo in 969, had inherited the powers of the seventh imam. Fatimid Shi'ism was a powerful, missionary force in the eleventh century, although it also produced further schismatic forms in the Druzes and the Nizari Isma'ilis or Assassins.

Divisions in Medieval Christendom

In the fourth, fifth and sixth centuries Christian theologians had grappled with the startling idea that Christ was both God and man. Most of them came to agree that He is at the same time the one God and a true human being, who has preceded the rest of mankind to heaven; but others, who formed the Nestorian and various Monophysite churches, found this concept impossible to accept. Many Monophysites were to be found in Egypt and the Levant. The Nestorians spread throughout Asia. In eleventh-century Europe another debate, this time over the nature of authority in the church, was beginning to divide Catholics of the 'Latin' tradition under the leadership of the popes in Rome from Orthodox of the 'Greek' tradition under the leadership of the patriarchs of Constantinople. Although there was probably no conception of schism on either side for another century, relations between Rome and Constantinople were deteriorating. At a time when there was a shift in the balance of power in favour of western Europe, they were undermined further by the policies of radical church reformers who had seized control of the papacy. To these western churchmen reform could only come about if the papacy, the church's central organ of government, was free and actively engaged. 'Liberation' of the church was their battle-cry and it would not be difficult to extend this to a summons to liberate eastern Christians from the Muslim yoke.

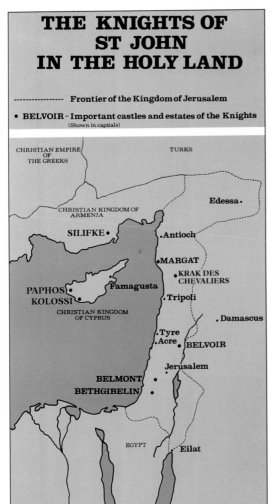

**THE KNIGHTS OF
ST JOHN
IN THE HOLY LAND**

------------ **Frontier of the Kingdom of Jerusalem**

• **BELVOIR** – **Important castles and estates of the Knights**
(Shown in capitals)

CHRISTIAN EMPIRE
OF
THE GREEKS

TURKS

CHRISTIAN KINGDOM OF
ARMENIA

Edessa•

SILIFKE •

•Antioch

•**MARGAT**

• **KRAK DES
CHEVALIERS**

PAPHOS•
KOLOSSI •

•Famagusta

•**Tripoli**

CHRISTIAN KINGDOM
OF CYPRUS

•Damascus

•**Tyre**
•Acre•
BELVOIR

Jerusalem

BELMONT •
BETHGIBELIN •

EGYPT

•**Eilat**

held the whole of the Levantine coast from Alexandretta in the north to Gaza in the south, with the sole exception of the city of Ascalon and its territory, which fell to them in 1153. Reinforcements who wished to travel overland now had an assured route once they had crossed Asia Minor. Smaller contingents, which it was practicable to transport by sea, had a more secure passage, because the Egyptian galley fleet, the only really effective military arm left to the Fatimid caliphs in Cairo, was deprived of ports to take on water and did not have the range to operate effectively against the northern Mediterranean shipping lanes. The settlers embarked on a massive building programme: of port facilities, castles, town fortifications, monasteries and churches, above all in and around Jerusalem where, it has been suggested, they were trying to mirror the heavenly city in stone. But there were never enough of them to assure security, which was one of the reasons for the emergence of the military orders.

The Latin kingdom of Jerusalem and the other settlements established in the Levant – the principality of Antioch and the counties of Tripoli and Edessa – were by no means the only component parts of the Latin East, nor were they the longest lasting. In 1191 Cyprus was occupied and after 1204 Greece and the islands of the Aegean. Although the Levantine coast was lost in 1291, parts of Greece were held into the fifteenth century, Cyprus until 1571 and Crete until 1669. The conquest of so much of the eastern Mediterranean seaboard meant that, although Jerusalem and a large part of the Palestinian interior were lost to the Muslims in 1187, the settlers on the coast were in some ways more secure and less isolated in the thirteenth century than they had been in the twelfth. Something of a common civilization developed throughout the region and it is possible to speak of cultural capitals of the Latin East: Jerusalem in the twelfth century, Andravidha in southern Greece in the thirteenth and Nicosia

Jubail viewed from the fortified harbour (foreground). The citadel can be seen in the background on the right and the cathedral – the only crusader church still in Catholic hands – on the left.

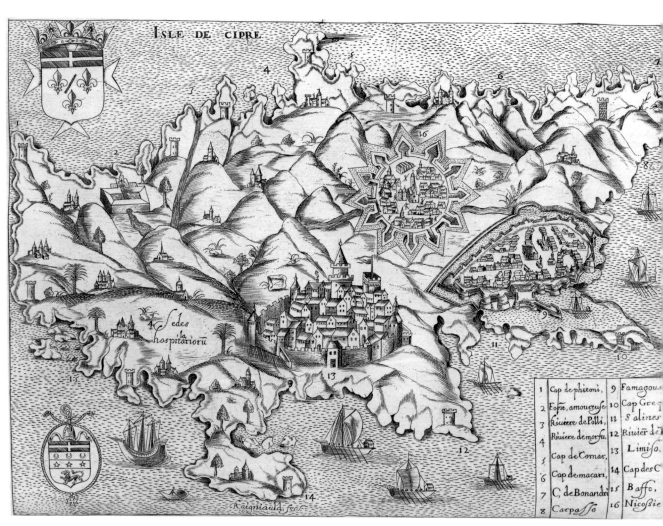

ISLE DE CIPRE

4 *Sedes la hospitarioru*

Raignauld, fec.

1	Cap de phitoni,	9	Famagous
2	Fonte amoureuse	10	Cap Gre
3	Riuiere de Polli	11	S alines
4	Riuiere de morfu	12	Riuier de
5	Cap de Cornar,	13	Limiso
6	Cap de macari,	14	Cap des C
7	C, de Bonandn	15	Baffo,
8	Carpasso	16	Nicossie

✠ 16 ✠

The cathedral of St Nicholas at Famagusta (now a mosque), a resplendent example of fourteenth-century Cypriot Gothic, built at a time when Cyprus was the cultural capital of the Latin East. After the loss of the mainland it was here that the kings of Cyprus underwent a second coronation as titular kings of Jerusalem.

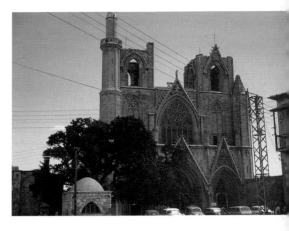

in Cyprus in the fourteenth. Shipping, particularly Italian shipping, which had developed rapidly in the twelfth century, bound the various settlements together, untroubled by Muslim seapower.

The region the westerners had occupied was prosperous. It was a major source of products in great demand in Europe, such as sugar and cotton. With a change in the Asiatic trade routes around 1170, it straddled for a time the most important trade route to the Far East, down which came highly valuable commodities like spices. Acre became the most important commercial centre in the eastern Mediterranean region and the taxation of goods in transit brought huge revenues to its government. The English chronicler Matthew Paris claimed he had been told by Richard of Cornwall, the king of England's brother who had been on crusade to Palestine in 1240, that Acre was worth to its lord the equivalent of the revenues of the English crown. The westerners were able to exploit the change in the trade routes in their favour because they had taken over sophisticated bureaucratic machinery from their Muslim predecesssors. After an early period characterized by violence and racial tension, they had settled down, like all conquerors, to make use of the instruments of government they found. Revenues in the countryside continued to be gathered by traditional methods. The tax-collecting offices at the gates, in the ports and in the markets of the cities were of standard east Mediterranean types, similar to those in other Byzantine and Muslim ports.

The patterns of Asiatic trade, however, changed again around 1260. Acre went into economic decline at a time when the threat from Islam, and the consequential expenses of defence, increased. The growing power of Egypt, now under Mamluk government, and the growing weakness of the Christians meant that the days of the kingdom of Jerusalem were numbered. After the last beachheads on the mainland had surrendered to the Muslims in 1291, Famagusta in Cyprus became the main entrepôt in western hands, although it was never to achieve Acre's eminence.

The island of Cyprus. A sixteenth-century engraving, showing (16) the capital city of Nicosia with its up-to-date Venetian fortifications, the cities of Famagusta (9) and Limassol (13), and the Hospitaller commandery of Kolossi (near 4). Engraving.

2

Knights Hospitaller

Christian monasticism was the creation of masters of religion who in the third century had withdrawn from the world to lead a spiritual life in the Egyptian desert, but the idea came to be widened to include those who lived in a way which combined 'withdrawal' with the active work of pastoral care or charity, which is why the word 'religious' is often used to describe those who share the belief that men or women can only grow spiritually if they are disentangled from earthly cares but do not necessarily divorce themselves entirely from them. The principles of monasticm reached the west in the fourth and early fifth centuries and it took many forms until an attempt at church reform around 800 led to the predominance of the rule of St Benedict (composed between 535 and 546), which was imposed on the dominions of the Carolingian emperors in a drive for uniformity.

The period of Benedictine dominance ended in the century between 1050 and 1150, when in an age of increased religiosity and older vocations Benedictine monasticism was not satisfying all aspirations. This has occasionally been described as a crisis for monasticism, but the old monasteries continued to flourish and there was actually a phenomenal increase in the numbers entering the religious life. It was, rather, a return to the norm after centuries of artificial Benedictine dominance, with a variety of expressions appealing to different postulants and benefactors. There was a movement within the Benedictines for a return to strict adherence to the original rule, which, it was believed, had been corrupted by accretions.

There was a new severe eremitism: the life of hermits or near-hermits. And increasing numbers of clergy wanted to live 'the apostolic life' under rules in which there was a special emphasis on pastoral activities. So, after centuries in which it seemed that only one type of religious life had been on offer in the west, there suddenly emerged a plethora of different forms, many of which are still with us today: Cistercian, Carthusian, Premonstratensian, Franciscan, Dominican – and Hospitaller.

The Hospital in Jerusalem

It is certain that the order of the Hospital of St John originated in a hospital (or hospice), which was already caring for pilgrims when Jerusalem was captured by the First Crusade on 15 July 1099. It is far less easy to establish how long that hospital had been in existence. The brothers themselves came to believe in a history that stretched back to a foundation by Judas Maccabeus, long before Christ, and even the popes seem to have accepted that their hospital had been the scene of many of the incidents in Jerusalem described in the New Testament. But although there had been periodic foundations of hospitals or hospices in Jerusalem – one was attested in the late ninth century, another in 1039 – it seems that none of these had a continuous existence until a Benedictine abbey called St Mary of the Latins, the only Catholic establishment in Jerusalem at the time, established a dependent hospital on ground just to the south of the Holy Sepulchre compound around the year 1080.

The early hospital must have been staffed, or at least administered, by monks from the abbey next door. It is probable that they were lay brothers and that they constituted the original members when the hospital broke away from its monastic parent some time before 1113. The name of their supervisor, Gerard, is known, although where he came from is a mystery. He went on to become the first master of the order. In an age of highly original founders of new religious institutions he must rank high among them, because the ethos of the early Hospitallers was a departure in religious thinking.

Their prime commitment was to the service of the 'holy poor'. A concern for the poor, of course, had always been a feature of Christian thought, but its radical expression around 1100 probably reflected the

Relic of the Blessed Gerard. A skull revered as that of Blessed Gerard, the founder of the order. It is now preserved in the Convent of St Ursula in Valletta.

The cloister of the abbey of St Mary of the Latins, the mother house of the Hospital of St John. Water-colour by Philippa Stephenson, *c.* 1923.

fact that, with economic advances in Europe and the rise of the towns, the urban proletariat was becoming more visible than it had been since the late Roman empire. The veneration of poverty as something evangelical reached its fullest expression in the ideals of St Francis a century later – although with him they involved the imitation of holy poverty in oneself – but in their abject humility and loving respect for the poor the Hospitallers foreshadowed the Franciscans. Gifts to the Hospital were made 'to the poor of Christ', of whom the master was both 'serf' and 'guardian': the grand master of the order of Malta still bears the title of *Custos Pauperum*. The brothers were also 'serfs of the poor'; their clothing, according to their Rule (composed around 1130), should be humble

> because the poor of Our Lord, whose serfs we acknowledge ourselves to be, go about naked and meanly dressed. And it would be wrong and improper for the serf to be proud and his lord humble.

They made no distinction between religions. In the 1180s their hospital in Jerusalem,

> knowing that the Lord, who calls all to salvation, does not want anyone to perish, mercifully admits men of the Pagan faith [Muslims] and Jews ... because the Lord prayed for those afflicting him, saying: 'Father, forgive them for they know not what they do'. In this blessed house is powerfully fulfilled the heavenly doctrine: 'Love your enemies and do good to those who hate you'; and elsewhere: 'Friends should be loved in God and enemies on account of God'.

To the Hospitallers the indigent man or woman really represented the person of Christ and should be venerated as such and from the first they realized their concern for the poor – and in particular poor pilgrims to Jerusalem, since they did not have many hospitals elsewhere – by caring for them when they were sick and burying them if they died.

There had always been some organized care of the sick somewhere in western Europe in the early middle ages, but for a long time there was a sense of impermanence about it. Public hospitals were more a feature of the eastern (the Byzantine and Islamic) world; they were occasionally established in the west after the fall of the Roman empire, but they did not last long, although there was a tradition of private hospitals, such as monastic infirmaries.

The continuous line of public hospitals started relatively late, but
by 1100 a movement dedicated to caring for the sick was under
way. Fourteenth-century England had 600 hospitals, most of them
small and containing fewer than thirty beds, although some were
very large: St Leonards at York could care for 224 sick and poor.

Medieval public hospitals were of two types. The first does not
really concern us, although there were examples of it in the Latin
east, especially a leper hospital in Jerusalem run by the brothers
of St Lazarus. It is significant that the one category of patients the
hospital of St John in Jerusalem did not admit were lepers. Leper
hospitals dealt with diseases that were thought to be incurable and
highly infectious, and they isolated the sufferers permanently from
the outside world, although usually in a tolerant and charitable
way. The institution would be run by a master, almost invariably
a priest, who was assisted by nursing brothers and sisters. The
patients were also regarded as 'brothers' and 'sisters' of the house,
which was a little self-enclosed religious community, in which all

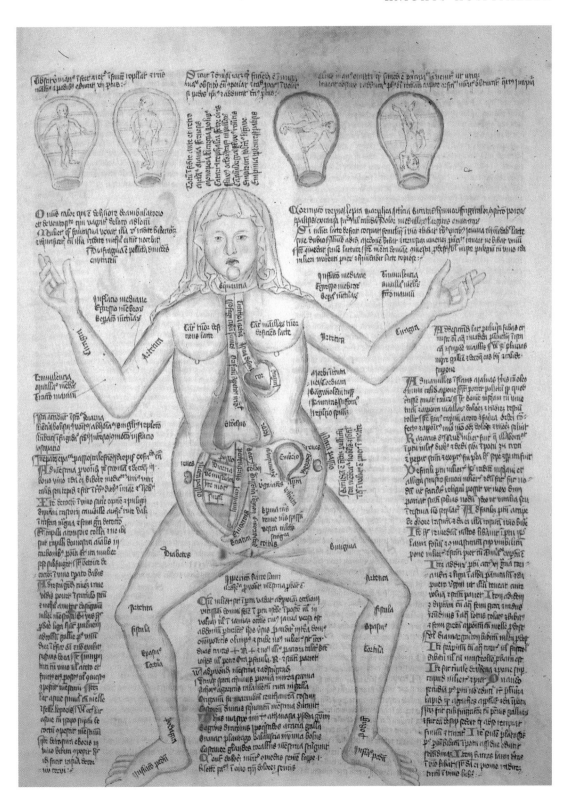

Physicians at a surgery.
One is inspecting urine, and
a variety of injuries and
diseases are shown by the
waiting patients.
British Library, MS Royal
15.E.2, fol. 165.

the inmates, as full members, had a say in the management of their affairs.

Hospitals of the second type were concerned with the treatment of diseases which were considered to be curable. The surgical techniques and medical treatments available to surgeons, physicians and nurses were relatively simple. Surgeons could perform superficial operations; for example for piles, ruptures and cataracts, or for the removal of nasal polyps. There was a knowledge of antiseptic (vinegar), which may have been introduced to the east by the crusaders. There was some understanding of the use of traction in the treatment of fractures. There was a primitive anaesthetic: a sponge impregnated with opium or mandragora and soused in hot water so that the patient inhaled the steam. There were various mercurial treatments for chronic skin infections. There was enthusiastic bleeding on almost every occasion, even on those cases when nowadays a blood transfusion would be prescribed. Everyone, however, knew there were limits to what could be achieved by surgery or treatment and most western hospitals, following the teaching of the great medical school at Salerno, relied on something else entirely. It was perfectly well understood that most patients would cure themselves in time if they were properly nursed, fed well, kept clean, warm and peaceful: hospitals like Santa Maria Nuova in Florence had separate sections for the delirious. The method worked: a hospital in Arras admitted between 2000 and 4000 patients a year in the period 1307–1336. Deaths averaged only 102 a year. On the other hand, one visitor to the hospital in Jerusalem in the twelfth century remarked with awe that sometimes at night more than fifty corpses were carried out; perhaps he was in the city during an epidemic.

A feature of Hospitaller nursing was this: because every poor man and woman *was* Christ, he or she should have not just good treatment but the best and most luxurious treatment possible. This was a religious imperative; it was also the application of the basic nursing principle that patients should be comfortable and contented.

The great hospital in Jerusalem, which had an enormous influence on the development of others, took in the poor, whatever their religion, nationality or sex. It could accommodate 2000 patients, male and female. When it was overflowing, the brothers' dormitory with its beds was occupied by the sick and the brothers had to sleep on the floor. If the sick had not the strength to admit themselves, the Hospitaller servants would search through the city and bring them in. On reception the Christian patients made confession and received communion; thereafter they seem to have been encouraged to receive the sacrament every Sunday. They were distributed in eleven wards, which were blessed with holy water every day. There were wards for sick women, who were looked after by female domestic servants; one was devoted to obstetrics. New-born babies were bathed as soon as they were born and wet nurses were provided for those whose mothers could not feed them through poverty or illness. Each ward was overseen by a brother whose business it was to assign the beds. He was assisted by twelve paid servants, whose duties included making the beds, looking after the patients, giving them water and towels and feeding them. Two of these servants were on duty in each two adjoining wards every night. They had to light the three or four lamps (besides the nightlights) which burnt in each ward from dusk to dawn, make the patients comfortable, call priests if they were needed and carry the bodies of those

Seal of the master of the Hospital. Reverse showing a patient in bed.

who had died into the conventual church. Every evening one of these servants would walk through the ward, a candle on the end of a staff in his left hand and a beaker of wine in his right, calling out continually, 'Lords, wine on behalf of God'. His companion would follow with a candle and a glazed jug of cold water calling out 'Water on behalf of God'. One of the servants would then bring hot water into the ward saying 'Hot water in the name of God'. After compline a tour of inspection would process through all the wards, led by a brother with a light and the rest with candles. Two brothers then joined the servants on night duty.

There were separate beds for the sick at a time when only the grandest lords had their own beds (and in the obstetrical ward there were little cots so that the babies should not be disturbed by their mothers). The beds had feather mattresses and coverlets, and the patients were provided with cloaks and sandals, so as to protect them when they went to the latrines. The bedclothes were changed every fortnight. Every Monday and Thursday barbers employed by the order washed the feet of the sick with hot water, removed hard flesh with a pumice stones and dried their feet with soft towels.

The diet provided was lavish. There were two kitchens, one common to both male and female sick, the other specializing in foods for patients with problems with digestion. At a time when very few people had white bread at any time or a meat diet, white bread was served to the sick, together with fresh meat on three days a week and an extraordinarily wide range of vegetables and fruits.

Four physicians and four surgeons, together with a number of bloodletters, were employed: the Hospitallers did not like entrusting the sick to outsiders. The wards were distributed among them so that each physician had

ABOVE. The fifteenth-century Hospital on Rhodes.

OPPOSITE. The building of the hospital in Jerusalem. Woodcut from one of the first printed editions of Guillaume Caoursin, *Statutes of the Order by the Chancellor* (Ulm 1493).

An order hospital. Fifteenth-century woodcut showing physicians at work on their rounds, in the background, and inspecting urine, foreground left, while a priest hears a patient's confession and a corpse is sewn into his shroud.

sole charge of the patients in his care. He was obliged to visit them each morning and evening to inspect their urine and take their pulses. On his rounds he was accompanied by two servants from the ward concerned, one to mix the lectuaries, syrups and other medicines, the other to show him the urine and clean the urinalia. The surgeons had care of the injured in Jerusalem and they staffed a mobile tented hospital on Christian expeditions against the Muslims. If the wounded could not be treated properly there, they would be sent on beasts of burden to the hospital in Jerusalem or to the hospital nearest to the battlefield. If there were not enough animals available to move them, 'the wounded mount the horses of the brothers[-at-arms] themselves, and the brothers, even the noble ones, return on foot', openly demonstrating that what they had belonged to the sick.

The order also provided services outside the hospital. When women in the city were too poor to clothe their babies, it sent them baskets of clothing. If a mother could not bring up a child, the master was informed. If sickness was the cause, he entrusted custody of the child to another. If the reason was poverty, he

✠ 28 ✠

De Hospitalitate.

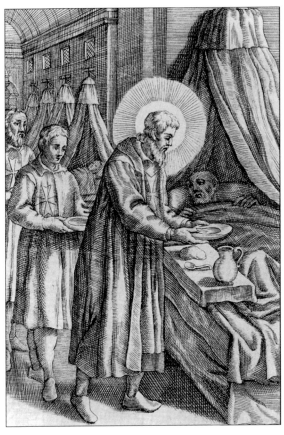

ABOVE. Almsgiving by the brothers of the hospital of St John of Jerusalem (1493).

The Blessed Gerard serving the sick. The scene is actually the Sacred Infirmary in Valletta, where the sick were served from silver dishes and beakers. Engraving from Bosio's *Historia della Sacra Religione di Ordine Hierosolomitani* (1570).

OPPOSITE. The ward of the Sacred Infirmary, Valletta. The brothers are serving the sick; a physician is taking a pulse; and another is examining urine. Engraving from the statutes printed for Grand Master Verdala, *Statuta Hospitalis Hierusalem* (Rome, 1588).

provided alms. If a mother through poverty or sickness abandoned a child, the hospital took it in, brought it up and educated it. The Hospitaller sisters were responsible for these adopted children, who were known as the 'children of St John'. The girls were taught a skill and when grown up could choose whether to serve St John or go out into the world. The wet nurses of the children of St John were paid, but were obliged to visit the hospital often to have the children in their care inspected. The sisters of the house would visit them and if their milk was failing would commit the children to other wet nurses.

The expenses of an establishment run so luxuriously and on such an ambitious scale were enormous. One has only to imagine the logistics involved in a hospital where the standards of nursing care were highly labour intensive and which catered for far more patients than any modern unit would consider admitting. Most patients would be sleeping in separate beds for the first time in their lives and would certainly never have eaten such good food

✠ 29 ✠

so regularly or have had such close spiritual supervision. Although it has been suggested that the hospital's organization into wards reflected Byzantine traditions and that the medicine practised in it was Arabic, its physicians seem to have been Latin Christians and there is no evidence that its standards and practices were anything but western. The nursing regime seems to have been Salernitan.

The Templars and Militarization

The Templars originated in Jerusalem during the winter of 1119–20, in an atmosphere of crisis engendered by a catastrophic defeat recently suffered by the Christians. A small group of knights, under the leadership of a noble from Champagne called Hugh of Payns, formed themselves into a brotherhood with the aim of securing the pilgrim roads to and from the holy places, which were still very unsafe. They took vows of poverty, celibacy and obedience and their establishment, approved by the patriarch of Jerusalem, was recognized at a church council which met in Nablus in January 1120. Their foundation was confirmed by the church at large in 1129 at a council at Troyes presided over by a papal legate, which,

Pharmacy jars from the Hospital in Valletta.
Left: Jug, with spout missing, for medicinal syrups and other liquids, Italian majolica, sixteenth-century.
Second left: Albarello, with arms of Grand Master Manoel de Vilhena (1722–36), and paper label, *sapo mollis*, soft soap, used as an emollient. Italian majolica, eighteenth-century.
Second right: Albarello, with the arms of Grand Master Philippe de l'Isle Adam (1521–36), for mallow with wax, also an emollient. Italian majolica, sixteenth-century.
Right: Pharmacy jar, showing the symbol for Aesculaepius, with a label indicating that it was used for spicella root, brought in from the Americas and used in the treatment of round-worm. Italian majolica, eighteenth-century.

Food Served to the Sick in the Hospital in Jerusalem

White bread (made from wheat provided by two villages in
Palestine), rye bread, corn cakes and chickpeas.
Wine.
Pork, mutton and lamb, chicken (both cocks and hens), doves
and partridges.
Eggs.
Fish.
Almonds, chestnuts, chickory, cucumbers, dried figs, grapes,
gourds, lemons, dried lettuce, Palestinian melons, parsley,
ears, plums, pomegranates, purslain, radishes and rock-parsley.

Never on the Menu (for Medical Reasons)

The flesh of breeding sows (because a general rule of medicine
was that the female flesh of humid animals, compared to that
of male ones was harder, grosser, more sticky and more
indigestible).
Shrimps, moray eels.
Beans, lentils.

Some of the Responsibilities of the Order's Provinces for Supplying the Hospital

100 pieces of cloth for making coverlets from the French
priories; 2000 ells of cloth for the same purpose from Antioch in
Syria; 2000 ells of fustian from the priories in Italy; 200 felts
from Constantinople; two quintals of sugar for making lectuaries,
syrups and other medicines from Tripoli in Lebanon and Tiberias
in Galilee.

exploiting a wealth of experience of the religious life available to
it, drew up a rule for them.

The support they had from the church cannot hide the fact that
the founding of this religious order, the professed members of which
took familiar vows, listened to the office and then rode out to kill
their enemies, was abhorrent to some. It is surprising that the section of clerical opinion which disapproved was not larger. In fact,
so small – or so discreet – was it that we do not even have the
names of any of the critics; we know only of their existence from
the reactions to their views in the writings of the order's defenders. A reason for this may have been that the Templars quickly
gained powerful support, not only from King Baldwin II of

Jerusalem, who with uncharacteristic generosity gave them part of his palace in the Temple compound to be their headquarters, and others in the eastern settlements, but also in the west. Endowments to them were soon being made in western Europe and their ideal proved itself to be immediately attractive to western armsbearers. Although most sons of nobles and knights still entered the ranks of the secular clergy or the conventional monastic communities, some of them found in the Templar life a way of expressing their longing for a religion more in accordance with the culture of the society from which they came than were the traditional and new forms of monasticism. The Templars foreswore the ostentation and glamour of the world, but there was in their ethos enough concurrence with the world's values to make it, and not simply the prospect of fighting for Christ in the east, appealing.

With the foundation of the Templars the crusading ideal was transferred to another plane. They and the brothers of the military orders which followed them were expressions of a development in religious life in the late eleventh and twelfth centuries, the

Mural in the Templar church at Grenac-sur-Charente. Like the Hospitallers, many Templars spent their whole careers in the west, managing the estates which provided the fighting convent in the east with funds. Their lives would not have been too different from the men who followed the religious life in other orders.

emergence of communities engaged in active works of charity, but their particular role, and the church's acceptance of it, was startling, because it was as unprecedented in Christian thought as had recently been the idea of warfare as a penance which underpinned it and had provided the basis for crusading. With the brother knights warfare as a temporary act of devotion – the function of the crusader – became warfare as a devotional way of life. Whereas crusaders were laymen directing their everyday skills for a time into a holy cause, these were religious as permanently at war as their colleagues in other more conventional orders were at prayer. But, like them, they and their apologists insisted, they were motivated by love.

> Like true Israelites and warriors most versed in holy battle,
> on fire with the flame of true love, you carry out in your deeds
> the words of the gospel, in which it is said 'Greater love than
> this no man hath, that a man lay down his life for his friends'.

The process by which the hospital of St John became a military order remains a mystery. No reference to a brother knight can be found before 1148 and that one is doubtful. It was not until the 1160s that a class of brothers-at-arms under its own officer, the marshal, makes its appearance in the surviving material, although it must have been quite large by then: the design of the castle of Belvoir, begun late in the decade and one among several fortresses held by the order at the time, allowed for a large conventual enclosure, which suggests a community with a significant number of brothers, although not all brothers-at-arms. The Hospitallers themselves never introduced a military element into their vows at profession and it was not until the 1160s that their dual functions of caring for the poor when they were sick and defending them by force of arms were defined by Master Gilbert of Assailly, an enthusiast for militarization whose reign ended in disaster.

In 1136 they were given the castle of Bait Jibrin (Behtgibelin) by King Fulk. The chronicler William of Tyre's account of the event leaves one in no doubt about the castle's strategic importance. In 1144, with the situation in northern Syria becoming very dangerous, Count Raymond II of Tripoli gave them Krak des Chevaliers and four other castles, which together comprised a strategically important section of his county's frontier with Islam. In doing so he created a march in which they were to enjoy the usual privileges of marcher lords, including a say in decisions on peace and

war and a right to spoil. There are, however, two charters record-
ing gifts made to the order much earlier, on 17 January 1126, in
the presence of six Hospitallers, one of whom was a brother called
Durand who used the title of 'constable of the Hospital'. Although
it has been pointed out that the title constable could denote a civilian office, there is no evidence that it was used in any other sense
than the military in the Latin settlements in the east. The grants
of January 1126, moreover, were made and witnessed by men who
had been encamped with a Christian army which was advancing,
or was just about to advance, into territory controlled by Muslim
Damascus. The presence among them of a Hospitaller constable
makes best sense if the order was making some sort of military
contribution to the campaign.

What did the constable do? What process led to the order having the capability to garrison castles and to the establishment of a
class of brothers-at-arms? It may be that in the late fifteenth century there survived a memory in the order, which cannot provide
us with dates but can tell us something about the course of events.
It is to be found in two forms, in both of them alongside a lot of
nonsense, including myths of the Hospital's biblical foundation and
an apparent misdating of the First Crusade, which must be why
they have been ignored. One version, in both Latin and French,
is in a historical introduction to the edition of the statutes made
by William Caoursin, the order's vice-chancellor on Rhodes, and
published in 1493. The other is related in some way to the first
and so may be a bit later. It must have been written by a Hospitaller
priest; perhaps an English one, since the manuscript, which is now
lost, was in England in the seventeenth century. In one account,
secular knights who had come to the east to serve for a few years
as an act of devotion attached themselves to the Hospital; in the
other mercenaries were employed by it. In both accounts, after an
indeterminate period, these men became incorporated into the
order to form the class of brothers-at-arms; in one the wearing of
the cross was instituted for them.

It must have been common for secular knights in temporary residence in Palestine and committed to its defence to offer their
services to some institution in or around Jerusalem. There were
secular knights attached to the Holy Sepulchre. Before 1127 the
Angevin knight Robert Burgundio of Sablé had been associated
with the church of St Stephen outside the walls of the city. In 1130
it was known that others were serving for fixed terms with the

ABOVE. The Templar castle of Tartus. The entrance gate, now a mosque.

Hall at Tartus.

Templars. There is no contemporary evidence for secular knights serving the Hospital out of devotion at an early date, although laymen were helping out in the hospital in Jerusalem from the first years of the twelfth century and noble pilgrims were still coming in the 1180s to work voluntarily in the hospital and its kitchens, sharing food and living conditions with the brothers. It would, however, make sense if, like other religious institutions in Jerusalem, the Hospital was benefiting from the attachment of secular knights serving for pay or, more likely, out of devotion. Their needs explain references from the 1120s to knights in the west leaving their horses and arms to the order in their wills. They would have been present in the army invading the territory of Damascus in 1126 and the constable could have been the brother appointed to look after them, being the only member of the order with a military function at that time. The next stage must have been reached some time before the first brothers-at-arms make their appearance in the sources. Clause 19 of the order's rule, which laid down that the cross should be worn throughout the order, is an accretion dating from before 1153. Its wording suggests that it was an early statute and it may be that the story associating the adoption of the cross with the establishment of brothers-at-arms was accurate. It is just possible to suppose that in 1136 the Hospital garrisoned Bait Jibrin with secular knights and mercenaries, but it is hard to imagine that it could have taken on Krak des Chevaliers and a substantial march in the county of Tripoli in 1144 without the appointment of brothers as commanders. It is probably not a coincidence that the entry of leading nobles into its ranks occurred at about this time.

In the thirteenth century James of Vitry, the bishop of Acre, believed that the Hospital took up arms in imitation of the Temple. The fifteenth-century memory within the Hospital suggests, however, that its militarization was less an imitation of the Templars, who before their recognition by the church at large in 1129 were in a kind of limbo, attracting support from western nobles but also hostility from a section of the clergy, than a result of a similar process. The Templars may themselves have originated in another group of para-crusaders. There was a tradition in Palestine later in the twelfth century that the earliest of them had been attached to the church of the Holy Sepulchre when in 1120 they formed themselves into an independent body. The development of a military wing within the Hospital may have been a further expression of the religious aspirations of these secular knights, which in one case led to the creation of a new order and in another, almost con-temporaneously, to the transformation of an existing one, the function of which had been entirely pacific. Something extra-ordinary was going on in Jerusalem in the 1120s: secular knights serving there temporarily out of devotion may have played a significant part in a process which led to the most original contribution the crusading movement made to the religious life.

The first reference in the Hospitaller statutes to the brothers-at-arms lists their function among the other charitable acts performed by the order; in other words, as an extension of the care of the poor. If the foundation of the Templars in 1120 marked a revolutionary moment, the adoption of a military wing by an existing order which had been established with an entirely pacific purpose is astonishing. It certainly worried the papacy, which as late as the 1170s was reminding the Hospitallers that their first duty was to the poor. It was the pressing need of the Holy Land, which put an end to such concerns.

A Hospitaller Estate

Nothing much remains of the Hospitaller compound south of the Holy Sepulchre in Jerusalem, except for an eleventh-century Byzantine church which they adopted as their first conventual chapel. Elsewhere in the city substantial ele-ments of a twelfth-century German church and hospital subject to the order survives; as does the ruined crypt of their twelfth-century church in their cemetery at Acheldamach south of the city, with the charnel pits once filled with the bones of the pious. But some idea of the quality of their buildings can be gained if one travels ten miles out of Jerusalem into the Judaean hills. Abu Ghosh was one of two places identified by pilgrims at the time as the site of Emmaus. There had been a Roman fort there, and then a Byzantine church built over a sacred spring, before a crusader shrine church was built, probably before 1140. It was in the hands of the Hospitallers by the 1160s. A short distance away is another of their properties, a

The mortuary chapel of the Hospitallers at Acheldamach. The site is associated with the potter's field brought with Judas Iscariot's blood money after his suicide. The chapel marked the site of the order's cemetery for pilgrims and the remains of the charnel pits, where the dead were laid, can still be seen.

✠ 38 ✠

twelfth-century rectangular building, constructed around a court-yard, to which the crusaders had given the name of Aqua Bella. It has now been identified as a hospital, because a large room on the second floor, open along its whole length with an apse at one end – a chapel – has been identified as an infirmary hall. It could have been a monastic infirmary for sick brothers or a small dependent hospital for pilgrims who fell ill on the roads up the hills to Jerusalem. A feature of Hospitaller history is the way their architecture found echoes over centuries: it has been noticed that a small turret chamber for ablutions at Aqua Bella has parallels in the late fifteenth-century hospital on Rhodes.

Abu Ghosh and Aqua Bella seem to have been dependent on the Hospitaller castle of Belmont nearby, which was constructed around 1150 and may be the first datable concentric castle, designed as such from the first and an inspiration for the great fortress of Belvoir, built by the order between 1168 and 1172.

OPPOSITE. Byzantine church of St John, Jerusalem. An eleventh-century Byzantine church, abutting on the hospital in Jerusalem, which served as the Hospitallers' first chapel. Water-colour by Philippa Stephenson, *c.* 1920.

Abu Gosh. This twelfth-century shrine church belonging to the Hospitallers stood over one of the sites believed to be that of Emmaus.

The Loss of Jerusalem

At the end of June 1187, one of the largest armies ever assembled by the kingdom of Jerusalem – 1500 knights and between 15,000 and 18,000 foot – was mustered at Saffuriyah, while a Muslim force of 12,000 horse and a great many infantry was encamped near Sinn al-Nabra, south east of the Sea of Galilee. The Muslim Sultan Saladin, who ruled Egypt and Damascus and had laboriously constructed a confederation of dependent city states in Syria and Iraq, was gambling on forcing an engagement with them; his record as a general leading the jihad or holy war against them had not until now been impressive. He decided to tempt them to move against him by sending detachments against the town of Tiberias on 2 July, while his main force remained in the hills to the west. This presented the Christians with a real problem. The king of Jerusalem could hardly leave one of his vassals exposed to Muslim attack, although he was strongly advised to do so, but to get to Tiberias he would have to march in the summer heat across a plateau with few sources of water. The plateau was nearly 1000 feet above sea level, whereas Tiberias was 679 feet below it. The last stage of the march, therefore, would involve descending over 1500 feet into the Jordan valley.

That stage was never reached. The Christians began their advance on 3 July and almost immediately came under attack from Muslim cavalry. There followed a two-day battle on the march, during which the Christians were pushed off the road into rough country to the north and had to camp and resume their march on 4 July without water supplies. Ferociously attacked as they crossed

---

Jihad

The *jihad* is a striving after perfection – in self, the community and the world – which was interpreted as a collective obligation to make war upon non-Muslims until they submitted to Muslim rule, whether as converts or as *dhimmis*, tolerated persons of certain recognized religions, including Judaism and Christianity. Between the *Dar al-Islam* (the Land of Islam) and the *Dar al-Harb* (the Land of War) there was a continual state of enmity, suspended by safe-conduct or truce. For most of the time most Muslims have not felt themselves obliged to be continuously at war with outsiders and some have reinterpreted *jihad* to mean an effort at interior self-development, but there have always been a few – and in times of crisis more than a few – who have answered the call to war.

An early fourteenth-century map of Acre by Paolino Veneto, bishop of Pozzuoli. In the centre the words *hospitale ecclesia* and *domus infirmorum* (the last two abbreviated) mark the sites of the administrative compound, church and hospital of the order.

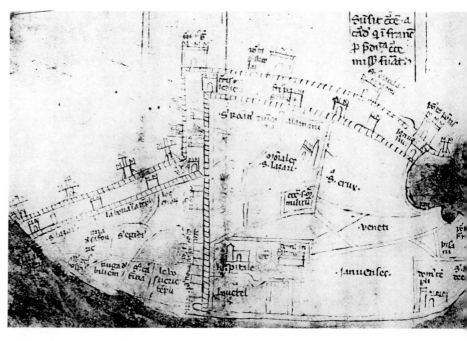

The so-called crypt of St John, Acre. The purpose for which this magnificent hall was used is not known. It looks, however, as though it was constructed before the expansion of the Hospitaller compound in the 1190s and must therefore have belonged to the conventual buildings on the site before 1187.

the plateau, the end came near two small hills, the Horns of Hattin, onto which the king and survivors had been forced. The Christian army was destroyed and Saladin ordered that all Hospitaller and Templar prisoners, whom he considered to be dangerous enemies of Islam, should be killed. His army then stormed through Palestine so that by September all the important ports south of Tripoli, except Tyre, had fallen to him. By 1190 only a few enclaves, including the Hospitaller castles of Krak des Chevaliers and Marqab (Margat), remained in Christian hands. To the south Hospitaller Belvoir held out until 1189, but Jerusalem fell on 2 October 1187 and the hospital of St John there became a Shafi'ite college.

Acre

Acre was the greatest city in the kingdom of Jerusalem in terms of size and economic

Acre. The newly excavated Hospitaller compound. Views revealing (*left*) a courtyard around which stood magnificent buildings; (*below, left*) an enormous sewage pit under a latrine tower, which may have been used by pilgrims, who were fed in the courtyard, as well as by members of the order; and (*below*) a line of warehouses, in which goods imported from Europe could be housed before distribution to the castles and commanderies in the east, and in which goods destined for exportation to Europe could be stored: in one of the warehouses, the excavators have discovered large quantities of sugar, still in pottery jars awaiting transportation when the city fell to the Muslims in 1291.

importance. It was recovered by a crusade led by Richard I of England and Philip II of France in 1191 and became the capital of the kingdom because, although it was back in Christian hands for fifteen years in the thirteenth century (1229–44), Jerusalem was now too exposed to be an adequate seat of government.

The order had properties in Acre before 1110 and a hospital which was at first in the eastern part of the town, although it was moved in the middle of the century to a new site to the north of the port area. On the recovery of the city, the military orders made the decision to establish their headquarters there. The Templars already had a fortress on the sea, which may have been the original Fatimid citadel. In the 1190s the Hospitallers were given permission to expand their conventual buildings, although for a time they may have moved their headquarters to the castle of Marqab in the principality of Antioch. The sensational results of recent excavations have shown just how spectacular their new headquarters in Acre were.

The brothers-at-arms were now lodged in a separate building in the suburb of Montmusard and the sisters were also housed in their own community. A vast complex was constructed round a great court. To the north was a range of warehouses, in which were stored arms, equipment and materal sent from the west, together with the produce of the order's Palestinian estates for export to Europe, probably through the use of Italian merchants as middlemen. A range to the west may have been the dormitory of the brothers-at-service, who did the menial work; at its northern end, and open also to the court, and therefore perhaps used by the pilgrims who congregated every day to receive alms, was a latrine block with interior plumbing, linked to the impressive system of sewers underground. To the east an enormous undercroft survives, although what the buildings above it were used for is not known, while to the south a fine hall, which must date from the earlier conventual buildings, was incorporated into another massive building. Outside the headquarters compound and to the south was

Mill at Kurdani. The Levant was the chief supplier of sugar to western Europe before the seventeenth century and the Hospitallers were involved in the production of sugar cane, its conversion to sugar and the export of sugar to the west.

the Hospitaller church, and beyond it the hospital, in which the traditions of twelfth-century Jerusalem were maintained.

The sugar factory at Kolossi in Cyprus. It and the sugar mill at Kurdani are examples of the industrial activities of the knights.

The Defence of the Holy Land

The popularity of the road the Templars and Hospitallers had taken is demonstrated by the way others soon followed them. These military orders included those of Calatrava, Santiago, Alcantara, St Mary of the Germans (the Teutonic Knights), St Thomas of Acre, Montjoie, St George, the Brothers of the Sword, S. Stefano and possibly St Lazarus. But the Hospitallers shared with the Templars, and to a lesser extent with the Teutonic Knights, the main burden of the defence of the settlements in Palestine and Syria. They took part in campaigns, helped to defend the larger cities and garrisoned and maintained castles, including some of the largest. These military functions were carried out by a relatively small number of brother knights and sergeants. In the twelfth and thirteenth centuries most brothers, even brothers-at-arms, served in the convents which managed the European estates. It is unlikely that at any time there were more than 300 Hospitaller brothers-at-arms and perhaps rather more than 300 Templar brothers-at-arms in the whole of the region. So the orders were large-scale employers of mercenaries. Castles like 'Athlit, Baghras,

Baghras Castle, known to the Templars as Gaston, was the centre of the first great frontier march given to a military order. It controlled the Belen Pass through the Amanus mountains, north of Antioch. With the Belen Pass closed, armes marching from Cilicia had to make a long detour to the north before descending into northern Syria.

'Athlit Castle, or Chastel Pèlerin, south of Haifa and one of the most important of the Templar fortresses, was not built until 1218. The castle was evacuated on 14 August 1291, three months after the fall of Acre to the Muslims. It is built upon a promontory, at the neck of which there developed a town with a sizeable Christian population.

Belvoir, Krak des Chevaliers, Marqab, Safad and Tartus would have had their own small convents, where the brothers would have lived in religious enclosure, greatly outnumbered by the rest of the garrison: at Marqab possibly 1000 men. Even in, or perhaps because of, an increasingly defensive posture, the employment of professionals and the maintenance of castles was enormously expensive. When Safad was rebuilt in the 1240s the Templars budgeted for a cost, over and above the income generated by the

Marqab (Margat) Castle.

Marqab and Krak des Chevaliers, the two most important Hospitaller castles in Syria, were both rebuilt in the aftermath of earthquakes in the early thirteenth century. In both there is, as at Belvoir, an area which corresponded to a monastic enclosure, because the number of brothers in the garrisons would be greatly exceeded by mercenaries. When one considers that these castles were being reconstructed at the same time as the new headquarters in Acre was being built on a lavish scale, one can only concluded that the cost to the order must have been stupendous.

Marqab (Margat) walls.

villages nearby, of 1,100,000 Saracen besants, the equivalent of between fifty and ninety million pounds today. Its annual running expenses were 40,000 Saracen besants (or between two and three million pounds). At that time the Temple had at least three castles of roughly the same size; so had the Hospital. Both orders had many smaller fortresses and shared in the defence of the larger cities.

They had the reputation of being hugely rich, and on paper they were. Their turnover was enormous, and it was this that enabled them to lend money, to become bankers – like many other institutions – and even in the case of the Templars to run the central treasury of the French crown; the Hospitallers performed a similar, but more spasmodic and understated, role in England. But their wealth was largely theoretical. This was partly because of the problem of getting it to Palestine and Syria, where it was needed. It could be sent in cash form or bullion, or changed into bankers' drafts. It could be converted into weapons, armour, horses and supplies before being shipped to the east with merchants or in hired vessels or even in ships the orders themselves owned. But in a world where the crossing of the Mediterranean had its perils, where too much cash stuck to too many fingers on a long journey, and where national governments could arbitrarily forbid exports and close harbours, one must assume that a large proportion of the cash raised in Europe never reached its destination. The logistical machinery required was elaborate and itself expensive. Periodically, after military disasters, a transfer of fresh manpower from Europe was needed. There were regular demands for equipment and horses. We also know that in the 1290s the Hospitallers were breeding warhorses on their stud-farms in Spain and herding the young animals north into meadow lands in France, where they were pastured and broken in, before being transported by sea to Cyprus. The generation of funds in both the east and the west required international management, even investment, policies.

Krak des Chevaliers

The fortress of Krak des Chevaliers, given to the Hospitallers together with a great frontier march in 1144, was one of a group of strongpoints guarding a valley which sweeps from the Syrian interior through Lebanon to the sea. It became a centre for operations against the Muslims in the region, and in its turn was attacked by them many times. In 1212 a western traveller reported that it was garrisoned with 2000 soldiers, the vast majority of them mercenaries. We know that in 1255 the order was proposing to have a permanent convent of sixty brother knights there.

Being in an earthquake zone, Krak des Chevaliers suffered damage several times. After a severe earthquake in 1202 the decision was made to remodel it. The original castle became the inner court of the new one, although a redoubt of three great round towers was added and the mound on which it stood was reinforced with a talus of dressed stone, within which was a fighting gallery. At least part of this inner court was the enclosed area where the conventual life was lived by the brothers: in it was their hall, with a portico constructed in the 1250s, and a large chapel, which

Krak des Chevaliers.

Krak des Chevaliers,
outer walls.

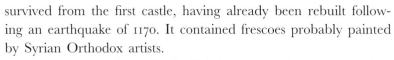

Krak des Chevaliers, interior
of the entrance ramp.

survived from the first castle, having already been rebuilt following an earthquake of 1170. It contained frescoes probably painted
by Syrian Orthodox artists.

An outer court, the walls of which incorporated many up-to-date
features, was now constructed. When the basic weakness of the
castle – that its strongpoint could be besieged by its own outer
walls – became apparent, the gate was reinforced and a U-shaped
ramp, dominated by obstacles and towers and leading straight to
the inner court, was built to a design which seems to echo that
planned in the previous century at Belvoir. But this did not really
provide an answer, as the deficiencies in the castle demonstrated

OPPOSITE. Plan of Krak des
Chevaliers, from
P. Deschamps, *Crac des
Chevaliers* (Paris, 1934).

✠ 48 ✠

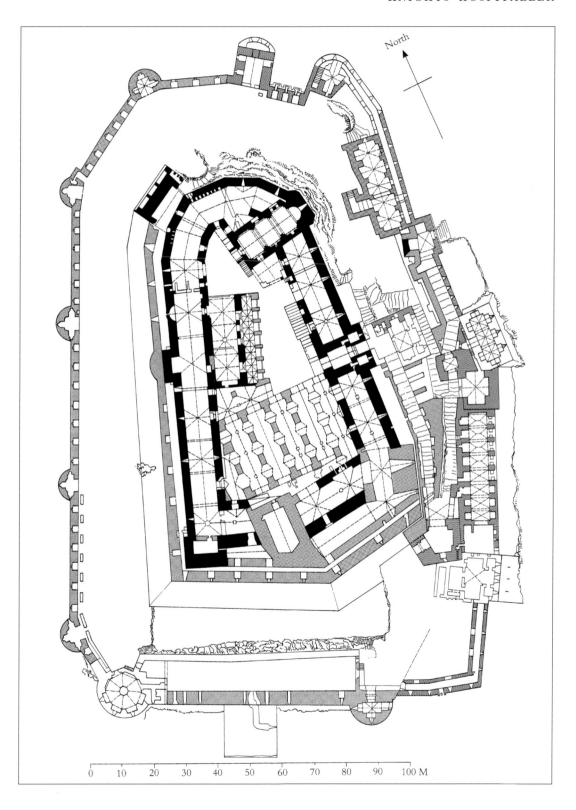

North

0   10   20   30   40   50   60   70   80   90   100 M

✠ 49 ✠

when the Mamluk Sultan Baybars came before before it on 3 March 1271. It did not take long to fall. By the 30th of March Baybars's troops had penetrated the outer court. The garrison surrendered on 8 April.

Crisis

From 1260 onwards the Mamluk rulers of Egypt systematically reduced the area of the Levant in Christian hands, destroying ports and castles for which they had no use and garrisoning others, so that an ever-tightening ring of forts enclosed the settlements. On 5 April 1291 a huge army, methodically prepared with an impressive siege-train, arrived before Acre. By 8 May the outer fortifications were so damaged that they had to be abandoned and on the 18th the defenders were overwhelmed by a general assault. By that evening only the Templar fortress-convent by the sea remained in Christian hands and ten days later, undermined by the Muslims, it collapsed, burying defenders and attackers alike in its fall. The losses suffered by the military orders were severe: the master of the Temple and the marshals of the Temple and the Hospital were dead, and the master of the Hospital was gravely wounded. Tyre was abandoned on 19 May. Sidon's sea-castle held out until 14 July. Beirut surrendered on 31 July and Tartus and 'Athlit were evacuated by the Templars on 3 and 14 August. Apart

The sea-castle of Sidon from the sea, enlarged by the Templars when they bought the lordship, south of Beirut, in 1260. It was in Sidon that they elected a new leader after the previous master had been killed in the fall of Acre in May 1291. They abandoned the sea-castle for Cyprus two months later.

from Templar garrisons at Roche Guillaume in the far north and on the tiny island of Arwad, within sight of the coast at Tartus, which held out until 1299 and 1302 respectively, and a shadowy vassal status enjoyed for some years by the lords of Jubail, Catholic rule in Palestine and Syria was over.

The military orders were unusual religious institutions in that they were not run by priests but by brother knights who were not and could not be ordained. Although their administrations were complex and efficient, they were managed by rather simple and uneducated men who did not have the sophistication to meet a new crisis that threatened to overwhelm them. They had already been facing increasingly hostile criticism. In 1274 there had been a proposal to combine all of them into a single body which, it was thought, would be more effective than they were individually. Although the idea was dropped when the kings in Spain leapt to the defence of their own national institutions – Santiago, Calatrava and Alcantara – it was revived and was on the agenda of every archiepiscopal synod in 1291. Jerusalem had been lost for good and the Christian hold on what was left of Latin Palestine was being progressively loosened. It is not surprising that the Templars and Hospitallers, who were associated in people's minds with the defence of the Holy Land, came to be blamed for allowing the catastrophe of its loss. Nor is it surprising that when the Christians were finally driven out the Templars should have faced renewed attack, although it took a form no one expected.

When they were driven from the mainland, the Templars and the Hospitallers retired to Cyprus, which had been in western hands for a century, and the Teutonic Knights to Venice. For about a decade the Templars toyed with the idea of occupying a beach-head on the Syrian coast, using Arwad as a jumping off point, but, unlike the Hospitallers and Teutonic Knights, they had lost their way. Periods of aimlessness and uncertainty can strike all great corporations, but it was unfortunate that such a period coincided with a ruthless and violent attack upon them. Early on the morning of Friday 13 October 1307 all the Templar brothers in France, including Grand Master James of Molay, were arrested by the French government. They were interrogated during the following six weeks and many of them were tortured. Almost all of them, including the grand master, confessed to an extraordinary list of crimes, including the denial of Christ, idol-worship and homosexuality.

The Templars were subject only to papal jurisdiction. Their

arrest by officers of the French crown, even if these claimed to be acting in the name of the inquisition, was an affront to the papacy, but the pope was in a weak position politically and the reports of the confessions weakened him further. All he could do was to order the arrest of the Templars himself and initiate proceedings, which became episcopal enquiries, throughout the rest of Christendom. Although James of Molay retracted his confession when interviewed by two cardinals, his brothers in France, who were tortured again, repeated their admissions. When two of their priests began to organize a more effective defence, the French government burnt fifty-four Templars in a field outside Paris, after which the defence not unnaturally collapsed. Outside France the enquiries gathered nothing substantial, but by the time a general council of the church met at Vienne in 1311 the pope was convinced that, whether guilty or not, the Temple was now so compromised that it could no longer perform a useful function. In the spring of 1312 it was suppressed and its properties were granted to the Hospital. On 18 March 1314 James of Molay and Geoffrey of Charney, the commander of Normandy, both of whom had continued to protest their innocence, were burnt at the stake.

The order cannot have been guilty of the crimes imputed to it. It was not a secret society but a large and well-known order of the church which could not have engaged in such bizarre practices without stories leaking out. The verbatim records of the commissions of enquiry suggest that, amid the maelstrom of innuendo and rumour that followed the arrest, no hard evidence came to light of anything other than the occasional case of homosexuality. In such a large body of celibate men it would have been surprising if there had not been a few such cases. King Philip IV of France was suffering from what amounted almost to religious mania and this was exploited by his ministers, who on several occasions concocted the strangest stories for his fevered brain to work on. The Templars were rich in estates and the French government was short of cash, while the king may also have been persuaded that he was bringing about a de facto union of the

The burning of the Templars. A late fourteenth-century representation of the burning of James de Molay, grand master of the Templars, and Geoffrey of Charney, the preceptor of Normandy, on 18 March 1314. British Library, MS Royal 20.C.VII, fol. 48.

Head of St John the Baptist, Templecombe Church, Somerset. The bizarre accusation that the Templars worshipped an idol in the form of a head has not ceased to fascinate the public, with extraordinary results. This head painted on a board from the parish church of the Templar commandery of Templecombe has been produced as evidence for idol-worship. But Templecombe was one of the many Templar properties taken over by the Hospitallers and this clearly dates from their period, because the 'head' is that of their patron, St John the Baptist, on a charger.

great military orders, because at the same time as the Templars were being crushed he was showing favour to the Hospitallers. The charges against the Templars look as though they had been constructed with an eye to public opinion. They opened with articles relating to their alleged denial of Christ as God, the crucifixion and the cross. The brothers were accused of spitting on a crucifix at their reception into the order, of trampling it underfoot and of urinating on it. In any Christian society these charges would have been horrific and sensational, but they also suggested that crusading theory and traditions, to which the authority of Christ and the image of the cross were central, were being challenged fundamentally. They were publicized widely by the French government and the public was presented with the appalling picture of a prestigious order, which claimed to embody in regular religious form the ideals of the crusade, blasphemously denying its central tenets.

One cannot get away from the fact that nearly all the Templars in France confessed. Coming from minor, provincial noble families, most of the knights had made profession in their teens and were barely literate; the grand master himself admitted that he was unlettered. Although lions in battle, these conventional, rather inadequate men could not cope with ruthless governmental terror; the same reactions were discernible, with a few honourable

Kolossi, Cyprus. Castle and aqueduct. Engraving from the *Graphic* (1883).

exceptions, in the English Hospitallers' responses to the dissolution of their priory by King Henry VIII in 1540.

After the suppression of the order most of the surviving Templars ended their days as pensioners in other religious establishments. Their property was transferred to the Hospitallers. The Templar myth – that the order survived as a coherent underground body to feed its way into esoteric associations like Freemasonry – seems to have been fabricated in Germany around 1760 by men who built on earlier romantic and invented associations of the Freemasons not with the Templars but with crusaders in general and with the Hospitallers. So successful were they that by the 1770s Templarism was firmly established in German Freemasonry. This is well known, but it is amazing how often it has to be pointed out that the Templar myth is an eighteenth-century German invention. The Templars were extraordinary as the members of the first Christian fighting religious order and, as such, they are historically important. They were good and disciplined soldiers and relatively good administrators. They were members of a large and influential religious order at a time when the church was at the height of its power. But in most respects they were really very ordinary. It was the bizarre nature of the accusations hurled at them by a ruthless government presided over by an eccentric king which laid the foundations on which their myth came to be built.

3

An Order of the Church

The Hospitallers were members of a religious order, restricted by vows of obedience and celibacy, subject to a rule of life which was strictly enforced. They were bound, like any religious, to fast at given times of the year and to attend mass and the customary monastic hours. It seems that, like the Templars, they were considered to be illiterate and were permitted to repeat paternosters over and over again while their priests sang the office. They were – and still are – greatly attached to their religion in its traditional forms. They fostered veneration of their own saints – especially Hugh of Genoa, Ubaldesca, Fleur and Toscana – and devotion to the Blessed Virgin Mary and St John the Baptist. They were greatly attached to their relics. They seem to have lost most of their original collection at Acre – the relics from Palestine preserved in Valletta are those they inherited from the Templars – but while on Rhodes they had acquired the two which were to become their most precious: the miraculous icon of Our Lady of Phileremos, which was housed in its own chapel in their conventual church in Valletta; and the baptizing hand of St John, which was placed in the oratory of that church. The icon and the baptizing hand were sent to Russia after the fall of Malta to Napoleon, were transferred to Belgrade after the Russian Revolution and are now in Montenegro.

The brothers may have been conventional in their religion, but most of them were very pious and some were profoundly so. The brother knight Fra Sabba di Castiglione's touching little book of advice

A group of Hospitallers, distinguished by their black cloaks with eight-pointed crosses on them, in an early fourteenth-century manuscript of an account of the conquests of Saladin. Bibliothèque Royale, Brussels, Cabinet des Manuscrits, no. 11.142, fol. 1.

OPPOSITE. The Crucifixion, from the Rhodes Missal. One of the centre pages of the missal commissioned for the order on Rhodes by the grand prior of St Gilles, Charles Aleman de Rochechinard, in 1504. He also commissioned great silver statues.

Breviary belonging to the church of St John the Baptist in Frankfurt. Fourteenth century, with a later inscription saying that the book ought to be looked after carefully on account of its antiquity.

St John the Baptist and the Presentation of Christ in the Temple. The late fifteenth-century Weston triptych, of which only two wings are known to survive, has the coat-of-arms of John Weston, prior of England and admiral of the galleys, 1476–89. His arms look as if they have been added later, but restoration showed that they are near contemporary. On either side of the Baptist's feet two other coats-of arms have been painted over with grass and flowers. It is believed that this painting was originally in the church of St John at Clerkenwell, as it is said to have been in England since the Reformation.

✠ 57 ✠

OPPOSITE. The Burning of the Bones of St John, late fifteenth century. This painting contains all the narrative elements of the story of the finding and fate of the bones of St John the Baptist, the patron saint of the Hospitallers. The painter is known as Geertgen van tot St Jijn. He may even have been a Hospitaller brother, but certainly he worked for the Hospitaller commandery in Haarlem. The brothers shown are certainly portraits, probably of Haarlem and perhaps Utrecht Hospitallers.

TOP RIGHT. The Beheading of St John the Baptist, early seventeenth-century. Caravaggio's masterpiece hangs in the Oratory of the Hospitallers' conventual church in Valletta. The painter had escaped to Malta, after committing murder. He painted several commissions for Grand Master Alof de Wignacourt (his painting of the grand master hangs in the Louvre), and was made a member of the order. Following another murderous encounter, he fled Malta and was pursued, but was killed in a drunken brawl.

Apotheosis of a Knight. Old master drawing showing a knight of St John on a cloud in heaven with angels. The knights were great patrons of European art, from the former Hospitallers who became cardinals to those, now often anonymous, portrayed by Titian, Tiepolo, Raphael and many others.

to a nephew who had also entered the order, first published in 1549, is as spiritual and penitent as any work emanating from a Counter-Reformation order of the time. Although the conventual buildings in Valletta, which were at first rather austere, became sumptuously decorated and comfortably furnished, the atmosphere on Malta remained fussily puritanical to the end.

Brothers and Sisters

The exact date at which the Hospital broke away from its parent body cannot now be established, but Pope Paschal II was treating it as an independent entity by 1113. His foundation charter, *Pie postulatio voluntatis*, seems to have been composed in conjunction with a bull of confirmation for St Mary of the Latins, which suggests he was confirming a separation which had just taken place. In it he wrote to Gerard, to whom he referred as 'founder', that the European hospices were 'to remain in perpetuity subject to you and at the disposition of you and your successors as they are today'. So the master was already overseeing an international structure, which by the time of the rule, about twenty years later, had become a network of scattered convents answerable to Jerusalem. The rule laid down that all these 'obediences' should provide the central government each year with what became known as responsions: a third of the produce of their estates. While the Hospitallers had a military rôle in a few parts of Europe – Aragon for instance – the purpose of their provinces was to channel recruits, money and supplies to the fighting convents in the east: 'convent' was the term used for any community of brothers. The order was internally bound by chapter: a weekly conventual chapter in each house; an annual priory or provincial chapter; and a general chapter of the whole order. At these justice was meted out according to the rule and statutes (the statutory legislation of general chapters), *esgarts* (case law), *usances* (customs) and papal legislation for the order concerned. There could be appeals up the chain of chapters.

The Hospitallers could hardly have carried out the tasks they had given themselves had they, like other religious, been subject to the local powers and the interests of diocesan bishops. Their order had to be centrally run and they needed to be able to transfer men and resources from one end of Christendom to the other, across national and ecclesiastical boundaries. The Hospital and the Temple were the first true orders of the church, international

The castle of Silifke, of which Ferrand of Barras was castellan in 1214. Silifke was held by the Hospitallers for a comparatively short time, 1210–26, but its importance to them is demonstrated by the impressive castle which was constructed. It has similarities to Krak des Chevaliers, which had been rebuilt only just before.

institutions governed from a headquarters which could post members from place to place. They were the originals in a movement that later led to the Franciscans, Dominicans and Jesuits.

Between 1135 and 1154 the Hospital became 'exempt'. Exemption, a relatively new privilege which was being increasingly given by the popes to new religious congregations, was essential if an internationally organized institution was to be free from local interference. It gave freedom from the powers of the bishops, making the order concerned dependent solely on the jurisdiction of the pope. It was bitterly resisted by the bishops, with the consequence that in practice compromises were usually reached at local level, but it technically freed the body concerned from the power of the most important provincial governors of the church and it meant that its internal government was its own affair.

The Hospital and the Temple developed aristocratic structures in which the brother knights predominated. In the case of the Temple, which was a military order from the start, it is not surprising that its leading personalities should have been drawn from the martial classes, but the Hospital was different in that it originated as a purely pacific institution and always maintained the dual function of nursing and fighting. So the climb to power within it of the brother knights is of particular interest.

In the earliest Hospitaller communities there were few distinctions in the brotherhood, other than that between those who had been ordained priests and the rest. Many houses, including

---

Mobility: The Case of Ferrand of Barras

1180 A simple brother in the priory of St-Gilles; no more than fifteen years old.

1194 Serving in the east. He was probably one of the young brothers sent out to fill the gaps left by the losses to manpower in the late 1180s.

1214 Castellan of the new and important castle of Silifke in Cilicia.

1219 Marshal of the order, its chief military officer during the Fifth Crusade and afterwards.

1246 Returns to his homeland as prior of St-Gilles

1259 Combines his priorate with the office of grand commander of Outremer, with supervision of the order throughout much of western Europe.

1266 Absolved by Pope Clement IV from fulfilling his obligation as prior to visit the convent in the east 'out of consideration for his personal condition'. He must have been over a hundred years old.

(It is possible, but less likely, that the evidence relates to an uncle and nephew of the same name.)

the convent in Jerusalem, were double, containing sisters as well as brothers. The sisters in Jerusalem were relatively elderly; perhaps the Hospitallers preferred to admit widows. They looked after the children adopted by the order, worked in the kitchen and inspected wet nurses, but there is no evidence that they nursed – that duty was performed by female domestics – or that they had any sort of managerial role, even the supervision of the female wards, although the Hospitaller prioresses were to have important executive functions later.

Women shared in the new forms of the religious life that came into being in the central middle ages and among nunneries there was as much apparent variation as among male institutions. Churchmen, however, were convinced that it was not appropriate for nuns to undertake what even male chauvinists would now regard as such proper female tasks as nursing or teaching. The sole basis of the common life for nuns was becoming retreat and prayer and there was little scope for a practical woman in such a life of

Knight of Rhodes in military dress. These frescoes in the Baptistry in Siena Cathedral, commissioned from Pinturicchio, and show an older knight in his religious habit, with the white eight-pointed Hospitaller cross of profession, and the island of Rhodes in the background; and a young knight in the military dress, a surcoat with the arms of the order, the plain white cross on a red background.

Hospitaller nuns at Sigena. Hospitaller sisters lived at first in the same convents as the brothers, but from the later twelfth century they were being segregated into their own communities. The most famous of these was Sigena in Aragon, which survived until the Spanish Civil War.

penitence and contemplation. Variations in rule disguised a sameness in activity: the Franciscan nuns, the Poor Clares, may have been given the *privilegium paupertatis* by Pope Innocent III in 1216, permitting them to live without an assured income, but strict claustration was also introduced, for St Francis would not permit religious women to wander. The church's view was to remain consistent: teaching and nursing were not for the religious but for laywomen, who could join confraternities if they wished. Only in the seventeenth century did the Little Sisters of Charity get round the prohibition by never taking solemn vows.

In the twelfth and early thirteenth centuries there was also a growing feeling that mixed communities were unsatisfactory. There was a reaction against them and an attempt, even by those orders with them, to cast them off. It took a long time for the Hospitaller sisters to be completely separated – some remained attached to male convents, including one on Cyprus in the thirteenth century and the commandery of Genoa in the fourteenth. From 1177, however, those in Aragon, Bohemia, England, France and Italy were collected into separate convents of canonesses regular, devoted to prayer, where they lost, if they had ever had them, Hospitaller functions. A rule for the most famous of their communities, Sigena in Aragon, was written in 1188. Each Hospitaller nunnery was administered by a prioress. She was subject to the provincial prior, attended annual provincial prioral chapters and sent either to the east or to the priory the equivalent of responsions.

As far as the central convent was concerned, the sisters had been detached and housed in their own separate community in Acre by

1219. The catalyst for this development at the centre may well have been the loss of Jerusalem in 1187 and the move of the headquarters to Acre. This may also have affected the relationships between other types of member. At some time before the early thirteenth century the brothers had divided into brothers-at-arms, knights and sergeants, and brother priests. These all had votes in chapter and

The investiture of a sister of the order. A late sixteenth-century drawing signed by Cavaliere d'Arpino, showing the reception of a sister into the order by the master.

Pierre de Bosredon, a Hospitaller from Champagne, out hunting. This late fifteenth-century hours of the Virgin Mary were commissioned by Pierre de Bosredon. Many of the illuminated pages show his coat-of-arms and those of the order, and he is depicted in many of the scenes. This scene shows how a Hospitaller on his commandery could often be mistaken for any other country gentleman on his estate. Pierpont Morgan Library, New York, MS Glazier 55, fol. 125.

so were not unlike choir-monks, but there was also an under class of brothers-at-service whose role was similar to that of Cistercian *conversi*. The class of brother knights was visible and organized by the 1160s, but even as late as the 1180s, when it certainly contained a 'noble' element, it does not seem to have been especially distinguished from others in the order. All brothers, except the master who already had his own living quarters, still slept in a common dormitory on site. By the early thirteenth century the idea of a common dormitory must have been abandoned, because the statutes of Margat (Marqab) envisage the brothers having their own cells. The creation of a separate house, the *auberge*, for the brothers-at-arms presumably dated from the move to Acre; it was certainly in existence by 1230.

In the 1180s the wards of the hospital in Jerusalem were staffed by paid servants, but a decade or so later these servants were being replaced by brothers-at-service. So, at the same time as the knightly element grew and distanced itself from the rest, the number of *conversi* grew as well, perhaps to take on community tasks that the brother knights were reluctant to perform. The thirteenth century, indeed, saw a hardening of the caste system within the order. In the 1230s, in the mastership of Bertrand of Comps, who was later said to have done more for the brother knights than any other master, they were given precedence over brother priests; and in the second half of the century the mastership and all other great offices were statutorily confined to brother knights, who were defined as those born legitimately into knightly families. Brother sergeants-at-arms did not have any such conditions imposed upon them. The caste system hardened in the later middle ages, with elaborate proofs of nobility in both paternal and maternal lines being demanded before admission, although there were always regional variations and knights of gentry or even bourgeois origin.

The Grand Master's Palace, Rhodes. The master of the order had his own separate residence by the 1160s and in the thirteenth century seems to have resided in some style in the Hospitaller compound in Acre. His magnificent palace on Rhodes was destroyed in 1856 but imaginatively reconstructed by the Italians in this century.

The Master and Central Government

The order was ruled directly and personally by the master (later entitled grand master), who resided in Jerusalem until 1187, in Acre on the Palestinian coast until 1291, in Limassol in Cyprus until 1309, on Rhodes until 1523 and on Malta from 1530 to 1798. His authority was never unlimited and became gradually more constrained. On election, which was for life, he took an oath to

The Grand Master's Palace, Malta. Watercolour by Charles Frederick de Brocktorff, c. 1819.

maintain the order's statutes and customs, to direct the business with the advice of his brothers, to observe the ordinances of chapter general and to see that they were observed by his subordinates. He had powers of general administration, exercised supreme command on campaign, oversaw the finances, and convoked and presided over chapter general. His was the final court of justice and he had the prerogatives of absolving brothers from their duties and exercising mercy on those undergoing punishment. From the fourteenth century onwards his most important single administrative instrument was the council, which must have existed earlier, although there are no references to it. Alongside it were the great officers, the grand commander, the order's second-in-command in charge of the general administration of the eastern properties and the provisioning of the central convent; the marshal, the chief military official to whom all brothers-at-arms answered; the hospitaller; the drapier, in charge of the clothing store; the treasurer: the admiral, who managed the fleet; the turcopolier, who commanded

Processional cross of the order from France. Made of thin beaten silver on an oak core, this cross now has a much earlier figure of Christ. On its reverse is a once enamelled coat-of-arms of the prior of France, Pierre Ducluys, and the date 1527.

Chasuble of the order. Silk church vestment with the arms of Grand Master Raimon de Perellos (1690–97).

OPPOSITE. Rhodes. William Caoursin reading a letter from the pope to the grand master, who is probably attended by his council, congratulating the order on its successful resistance in 1480. From *The Siege of Rhodes* by Guillaume Caoursin, Bibliothèque Nationale, MS Lat. 6067, fol. 83v.

mercenaries and was later to be responsible for the coastal defences of Rhodes; and the conventual prior, who was the chief chaplain at the central convent. Then there was the convent itself, organized into seven, later eight, *langues* (or tongues), and the chapter general, to which came, or at least were supposed to come, all the 'capitular bailiffs', the provincial administrators in Europe. It had developed by the 1160s, although at that time it met irregularly; only later did it come to meet at five-year, then ten-year and then six-year intervals. Its powers should have been sweeping: it legislated for the whole order and was responsible for auditing the performance of the great officers at the centre and the provincial administrators in the west. At times it successfully limited the powers of masters, but it could not have the day-to-day controls available to the convent, which seems to have grown in authority at its expense. Indeed its fate in the early modern period echoed that of so many parliamentary institutions in Europe: it was not summoned at all between 1631 and 1776.

The Langues and the Auberges

The number of brothers serving at the central convent and its immediate dependencies, whether in Palestine and Syria, Cyprus, Rhodes or Malta, remained remarkably constant throughout the centuries: around 300 before 1291, and between 250 and 450 during the Rhodian period. About 540 knights and sergeants defended Malta during the Great Siege in 1565, but that was exceptional; there were 266 brothers on Malta in 1631 and 332 knights there in 1798. From the thirteenth century these brothers were being

The brothers at mass at the time of an earthquake on Rhodes in 1481. Bibliothèque Nationale, MS Lat. 6067, fol. 120v.

The Street of the Knights, Rhodes. Direct access for the brothers to the hospital was on the left. The auberge of France is on the right. Engraving from Eugène Flandin, *Histoire des Chevaliers de Rhodes* (Tours, 1864).

Auberges. The term, meaning inn or hostel, was first used in the thirteenth century of a house in Montmusard, the suburb of Acre in which all the brothers-at-arms lived in community. With the emergence of the langues, separate houses began to be allotted to each of them, so that brothers from the same European region could live together. The auberges of the langues were well developed by the fifteenth century.

OPPOSITE LEFT. The Hall of the Auberge of Provence, Valletta, Malta.

RIGHT. The Auberge of the Anglo-Bavarian Langue, Valletta, Malta.

grouped into *langues*, because those from the same region natural-ly tended to congregate and because advice was needed before the central government considered any action with respect to one of the provinces in Europe. The great offices at the headquarters came to be attached to the langues, being held ex officio by their *piliers* or heads. If one gets the impression of a cosmopolitan organiza-tion, as indeed the order was, it should be remembered that it remained predominantly French, even when its official language

OPPOSITE. The Auberge of Castile and Leon, Valletta, Malta, the finest work of architecture in eighteenth-century Valletta.

The Langues

Provence	The priories of St-Gilles and Toulouse
France	The priories of France, Aquitaine and Champagne
Auvergne	The priory of Auvergne
Germany	The priories of Germany, Bohemia, Dacia (Scandinavia) and Hungary, and the bailiwick of Brandenburg
England	The priories of England (including the Scottish and Welsh commanderies) and Ireland
Aragon	The castellany of Amposta and the priories of Navarre and Catalonia
Castile	The priories of Castile-Leon and Portugal
Italy	The priories of Lombardy, Venice, Pisa, Rome, Capua, Barletta and Messina

(A very strange late addition was the Anglo-Bavarian langue, comprising the priories of Poland and Bavaria.)

---

changed to Italian. In 1631 it consisted of 1755 knights, 148 chaplains and 155 sergeants, of whom 995, or almost half, came from the three French langues.

In the thirteenth century the brother-at-arms lived together in a separate building, which was already called an *auberge*. On Rhodes each langue was given its own auberge. The importance of these residential houses to the brothers is demonstrated by the way new ones were being built as soon as the knights reached Malta in 1530. The auberges survive today in Valletta as splendid reminders of the order's occupation of the island.

Provincial Government

The administrative systems used by the Hospitallers and Templars were very similar. This was not a coincidence – they developed at a time when certain forms of government were fashionable – and their similarities must have helped the Hospitallers to absorb the Templar estates in the fourteenth century. The basic unit of administration in both orders was the commandery or preceptory. At its centre was a conventual building, often the original manorial lord's house, with a chapel and a few other buildings attached, from which a large estate, or a scattered group of them, was run. The size of commanderies varied, depending on the amount of management involved: their area of responsibility could roughly correspond to that of a shire (in England), or to a diocese; even, in more distant parts of Europe, such as in Scotland, to a kingdom. At commandery level the early brothers – sometimes as many as twenty of them – lived as true religious in community according to the rule, but later in the middle ages manpower was concentrated on certain sites and some commanderies were held in plurality, while others were rented to secular farmers or were occupied by single brothers who, after a career distinguished perhaps by long service in the east, lived on them as country gentlemen. Commanders were usually appointed by their priors, to whose jurisdiction they answered. They were supposed to pay responsions, to keep a copy of that part of the prioral register which referred to their commanderies and to attend the annual chapter of the priory concerned. Two types of commandery were unusual, but the numbers of them grew throughout the middle ages. The first were commanderies of grace, bestowed on a brother for life or for a term directly by the central government. The second were *camerae*, in the personal possession of high officials of the order, being held in absentia and administered by an agent.

All commanderies, however, were grouped in provinces known

A French commander. Gabriel du Bois de la Ferté entered the priory of Acquitaine in 1660, having fought in the French army, he became captain of an order galley. He was renowned for his piety and good works. Engraving by Chereau.

A commander inspecting an order estate. Engraving from *Statuta Hospitalis Hierusalem* (Rome, 1588).

to the Hospitallers as priories, later as grand priories probably to distinguish the grand prior from the chief chaplain of his community who had an office with the same title, and to the Templars as provincial masterships. Priories were sometimes themselves gathered into even larger circumscriptions called grand commanderies, but these seem to have been ad hoc creations, abolished as soon as the problem they had been created to deal with had been solved.

Temple Cressing Barn. Two enormous barns, dating from the thirteenth century, survive at the Templar commandery at Cressing in Essex, which was taken over by the Hospitallers, together with most of the Templar estates in England, in the fourteenth century. The size of the barns, close to a navigable river and within easy reach of London, suggests that Cressing had been a depôt to which the produce of a group of Templar commanderies had been sent.

The Temple in Paris in the eighteenth century. This had been the headquarters of the Templars in France and 'one of the key financial centres of north-west Europe'. After it had been acquired by the Hospitallers, they transferred the seat of the priory of France to it. Engraving.

VUE DU PALAIS DU TEMPLE AUX CHEVALIERS DE MALTHE
C'est le Logement du Grand Prieur de France, et aujourd'hui Monseigneur le Prince de Conty Prise du côté de la rue.

THE PRIORIES OF THE ORDER OF ST JOHN IN EUROPE

At the centre of each Hospitaller priory a community managed the affairs of the province under a prior, who was a capitular bailiff, theoretically appointable by and responsible to chapter general, although often directly appointed by the master. Besides choosing the commanders, priors visited the commanderies in their jurisdiction, received brothers into the order and acted as channels for the transmission to the east of responsions, whether in cash or in commodities, and of recruits suitable for military service. Each priory contained a financial office under a local treasurer and had its own archives. While there was corruption and incompetence, the more historians look in detail at the Hospital's provincial administration the more efficient they find it to have been.

A prior was required at times to visit the headquarters to report to the master and attend chapter general. He would anyway be in constant touch with his opposite number on Rhodes or Malta, the pilier who was head of the langue to which his priory belonged, and with the central government. Many priors played important political roles in the states in which they resided but, whatever their responsibilities, they would never have forgotten that their functions were essential to the order's operations in Palestine and Syria, Rhodes or Malta, for it could never have run great hospitals, financed its mercenaries and galley fleet and invested in expensive fortifications without the resources the priors provided.

Donation charter, Sutton-at-Hone, Kent. The commandery at St John's Jerusalem, Sutton-at-Hone, was built up from many small donations of land. It may have been carefully put together by the Hospitallers' agents to form a viable estate. In this one, John and Margaret de Bec grant to God, the Blessed Mary and St John the Baptist and the blessed poor of the holy house of the Hospital of Jerusalem and the brothers of the same house in England at Sutton at Hone two pence a year. Manuscript.

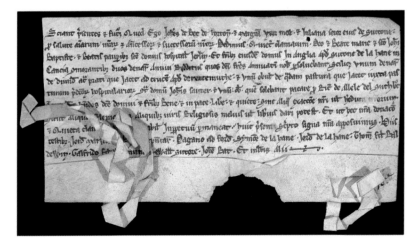

La Couvertoirade. One of a group of farming centres in the Templar commandery of Ste-Eulalie which passed to the Hospitallers after the suppression of the Temple. There was already a small castle, but in 1439 during the Hundred Years War the villagers were licensed by the prior of St-Gilles to fortify the town in 1439.

BOTTOM LEFT. St Giovanni de Pré, Genoa, the Hospitaller church in the city.

BELOW. St Jean-de-Luz. A fortified twelfth-century Templar church.

BOTTOM. Bubikon, Switzerland. A Hospitaller estate.

The Priory of England

The order began to receive gifts of land in England and in Scotland in the 1130s and 1140s, including the property at Clerkenwell, just outside the north walls of London, which was to be the site of the priory headquarters. Although in the twelfth century the Templars

Seal of the commandery of Godsfield, Hampshire.

Portrait medal of John Kendal. This is thought to be the first portrait medal of an Englishman. Kendal probably had it made in Italy, on one of his visits to the papal court as the order's ambassador, and on his trip round Europe to gather funds and support for Rhodes in the siege of 1480, the date of the medal. He was then turcopolier, in charge of the coastal defences of Rhodes, and later became prior of England, and was absolved of taking part in the Perkin Warbeck plot to overthrow Henry VII.

RIGHT. Late thirteenth-century Hospitaller missal. It is possible that this belonged to Joseph Chauncy, prior of England (1273–80), who had been treasurer of the order in the Holy Land and treasurer of England. He is represented kneeling at the feet of St John the Baptist.

seems to have been more favoured by English benefactors, the Hospitallers had twenty-eight commanderies by the turn of the thirteenth century and were beginning to play a prominent part in English politics. Several priors served as treasurers of the crown, beginning with Joseph Chauncy in the 1270s; a successor as both prior and treasurer was Robert Hales, who in 1389 was massacred by the mob in the Peasants' Revolt. By the

Prior John Langstrother waiting to be executed. Langstrother was executed after the Battle of Tewkesbury in 1471, having given his support to the losing side in this episode of the Wars of the Roses.

fourteenth century the priors were sitting in the House of Lords, where they came to rank as premier barons, and they were employed by the crown on diplomatic missions.

By 1338 the priory had thirty-four brother knights, thirty-four chaplains and forty-eight sergeants in residence in thirty-seven commanderies; not included is the great Hospitaller nunnery of Buckland, which still had fifty sisters in 1539. With the absorption

Ansty, Wiltshire. This shows the small parish church of St James, which doubled as the order's chapel. The building to the left was part of the commandery complex, and has been variously described as 'the hospice', and as an Elizabethan picnic house, but was almost certainly the court-house for the commandery. The lake was the commandery's fish-pond, to provide an important part of a monastic diet. Water-colour by Kay MacLaren Anderson.

OPPOSITE. Moor Hall, Harefield, Middlesex. This late eighteenth-century water-colour records an estate of the order which disappeared within living memory. It is shown in the 1338 report on the Hospitallers' property in England as a camera, one of those estates whose incomes were reserved, in this case to help towards the upkeep of the priory of Clerkenwell. At that time it had a house, three carucates of land, twenty acres of meadow, four pounds in annual rents, pasture for twenty cows, twenty young oxen and 300 sheep. The Hospitallers also had the parish church of Harefield. Moor Hall's house was damaged by fire in the 1950s and pulled down. The chapel, next to the house, was pulled down by the local council to make room for a football pitch in 1956. Water-colour by N. Smith (1794).

of the Templar lands the number of commanderies increased to fifty-nine in 1350, although many were held in plurality, which accounts for an actual reduction in number to nineteen by the time of the dissolution in 1540. Although it has never been established conclusively whether the Hospital of St John was *the* greatest ecclesiastical landowner in England, from the fourteenth century it probably was.

The Hospitallers in England might have survived the dissolution of the monasteries and religious communities by King Henry VIII, who, like his father, had been named protector of the order in 1511. The king seems to have toyed with the idea of converting the English priory into a royal institution not unlike the Spanish military orders and of using it to defend Calais. But the order resisted him and he was hindered rather than assisted by the outrageous chauvinism displayed on Malta by the pilier of the English langue, Clement West, whose extreme support for Henry's cause antagonized all the other brother knights. In April 1540 an act of parliament dissolved the order in England, conferring its estates on the crown. Although briefly restored by Mary Tudor, the medieval priory had met its end. It survived in name, shadowy and titular,

Torphichen, the Hospitallers' headquarters in Scotland. Granted by David I, it lay close to the royal palace at Linlithgow. Part of the Hospitallers' church remains, a solid, partly fortified building which had a hospice above its eastern section.

Dinmore Church, Herefordshire. The Hospitallers and Templars were given manors all down the Welsh Marches to protect against lawlessness and to provide shelter for travellers and pilgrims.

Above a gateway of the castle of St Peter, Bodrum, are the coat-of-arms of Sir Thomas Docwra, Grand Master Pierre d'Aubusson and the arms of the order surrounded by the Garter. Docwra was captain of Bodrum Castle in 1498, and turcopolier, before becoming prior of England, 1501–27. He refurbished the priory at Clerkenwell and built St John's Gate, which also bears his coat-of-arms.

on Malta. Two brother knights, Thomas Dingley and David Gunson, may have suffered martyrdom for the old faith. A few remained in exile, on Malta and elsewhere, but most conformed. The last resident grand prior, William Weston, died on 7 May 1540, the day the act of dissolution came into force.

Little Maplestead, Essex. A small round-naved church built by the Hospitallers, *c.*1245. This is a late example of this type of church, like the Hospitallers' much earlier church at Clerkenwell. They were also built by the Templars and crusaders. It is thought that the round nave derives from the rotunda of the church of the Holy Sepulchre in Jerusalem. The advowson of Little Maplestead, together with Sompting in Sussex, are held by the order of St John. Nineteenth-century engraving.

A View of the Inside of Little Maplestead Church.

The North View of Do.

The Plan of Do.

Quenington, Gloucestershire. Until very recently this was a place where one could clearly see the impact of the Hospitallers on a village. The fourteenth-century gatehouse to the commandery remains, as does the dovecote. In this country, unlike other parts of Europe, no one place remains where one can see all the elements of a Hospitaller or Templar commandery, but the different parts survive in different sites round the country.

Sutton-at-Hone, Dartford, Kent. The order's chapel in the right wing of the house survives in this National Trust house.

Temple Balsall, Warwickshire. A former Templar, then Hospitaller, site that today retains one of its original purposes. This pair of cottages were once a hall-house of the Templars, of which there is at least one other example at Foulbridge in Yorkshire. The Hospitallers greatly enlarged the church nearby. A charity still provides almshouses on the site.

Swingfield, near Folkestone, Kent. A large commandery, close to main ports, and to pilgrimage routes to Canterbury and often used as a resting post for important travellers. The chapel still survives, under the care of English Heritage. This nineteenth-century engraving shows it in use as a farm.

Temple Church, London. The round-naved church of the Templars' second London headquarters, consecrated at the same time as the Hospitallers' priory church at Clerkenwell, in 1185. The Hospitallers took over the site when the Templars were dissolved, and leased it out to apprentice lawyers, hence the Inner and Middle Temples. Engraving, 1807.

✠ 85 ✠

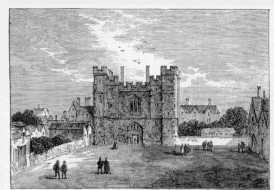
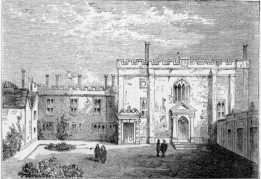

THE MONASTERY OF ST. JOHN OF JERUSALEM, CLERKENWELL
THE GATE FROM THE WEST.   GENERAL VIEW FROM THE NORTH-EAST.   THE CHAPEL FROM THE SOUTH.

ABOVE. The priory of Clerkenwell. Taken from Wenceslaus Hollar's 1656 engraving, this nineteenth-century version shows us how many of the priory's important buildings survived, which they did until the late eighteenth century. St John's Gate, built in 1504, is shown top left, and looks taller than it does today, as the ground level in this part of London has risen considerably. Top right shows the priory church which had already lost its nave after Protector Somerset dismantled both it and the great bell-tower, a tourist sight of early sixteenth-century London. Below can be seen three original windows of the priory church, which still exist today. To the right is one of the great halls of the priory.

BELOW. South chapel of the crypt of the priory church, Clerkenwell. This was an early building on the site given to the Hospitallers by Jordan de Briset, an Anglo-Norman knight in about 1140. The church above had a round nave, like the interior of the

church of the Holy Sepulchre in Jerusalem and like the nearby Temple church. The crypt was extended in about 1185.

RIGHT. St John's Gate. Built by Sir Thomas Docwra in 1504, this probably replaced the first gateway at the end of St John's Lane, very close to the boundary of the City of London.

✠ 86 ✠

Henry VIII's gun. Grand Master de l'Isle Adam came to England in 1528 to raise support for the order, after the loss of Rhodes. He met the king, who then gave the order nineteen cannons, with his arms and those of the grand master on them. One survives. This cannon was captured by the Turks, who seem to have dropped it into the harbour at Famagusta, where it was dredged up this century and presented to St John's Gate.

Henry VIII's warrant for the disposal of the lead off the priory buildings. Henry took all the order's properties in England into crown hands and the Court of Augmentations sold them off for the crown's financial profit. One member of the court was an ex-knight of St John, Ambrose Cave, who managed to sell a few of them to the families of other ex-knights, who were then able to worship in the old faith in their own private chapels. Henry's warrant, signed in his own hand across the top, authorized the removal of lead from the priory, but this was never done. He used the buildings to store his 'toils and tents for hunting and for the warres' and then gave it to his daughter, later Mary I, to have as her own palace.

BELOW. Charter of Philip and Mary restoring the order. Queen Mary, a Catholic, restored the order in 1557. This charter grants back to the Hospitallers many of their English properties, and gives detail of the tenants. Manuscript.

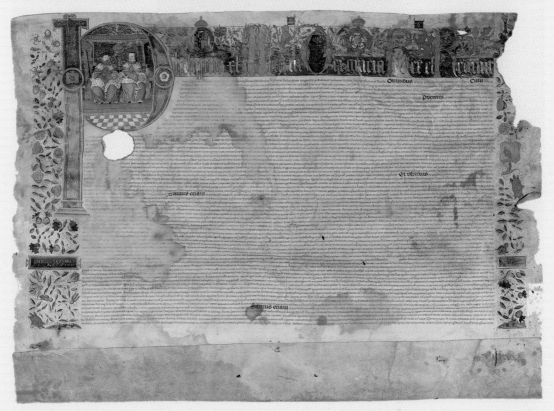

Andrew Wise. The dissolution by Henry VIII and the brief restoration of the order in England under Mary Tudor, and its eventual suppression under Elizabeth I, did not deter the order in Malta from appointing English priors, although this became in later centuries a matter of title. Andrew Wise, an Irishman, was made prior of England, although he lived all his life in exile. Oil painting.

Part of the tomb of Sir William Weston. William Weston, who fought at the Siege of Rhodes and lost a finger there, was prior when Henry VIII dissolved the order in England. He was not allowed to be buried in his own priory church and was buried in the parish church of Clerkenwell, St James. His tomb was opened, when the parish church was rebuilt, and for a brief moment his embalmed body was seen. He was tall and wearing robes.

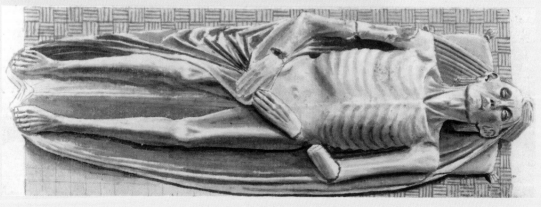

4

Rhodes and Malta

Nothing is clearer than the speed with which the Teutonic Knights and the Hospitallers reacted to the catastrophe that befell the Templars. In the same year, 1309, the grand master of the Teutonic Order took up residence at Marienburg in Prussia, and the Hospital of St John moved its headquarters to the island of Rhodes, just off the coast of Asia Minor and in the front line of the war against Islam. Although both orders were to face severe difficulties during the fourteenth century – the Teutonic Knights were lucky to escape suppression after a scandal had broken out in Livonia (Latvia) and the Hospitallers faced constant criticism and demands for reformation from the papal curia – they pursued the same policy of demonstrating to public opinion that they were positively engaged on Christendom's behalf. In doing this they developed a new kind of commonwealth, the order state, which had two features. First, it was a theocracy, governed by an elite class of soldiers who had taken full religious vows, originated from outside the state's boundaries and isolated themselves from the population. The rule of the Hospitallers on Rhodes and Malta (and of the Teutonic Knights in Prussia) was generally benevolent, but the indigenous population was kept at arm's length. Secondly, although theoretically defensive – Christian holy war required a just cause

SMYRNA

LEROS
BODRUM
CALYMNOS
FISCO
COS
NISYROS
SYMI
TELOS
LIMONIA
RHODES
KALKIA
RHODES
LINDOS
CASTEL
ROSSO

CARPATHOS

RHODES
and the Castles
of the Order of St. John

RHODES
KREMASTI
VILLANOVA
PHILERIMOS
PHANES
KOSKINOU
KALAVARDA
SALAKOS
KASTELOS
ARCHANGELOS
PHERACLOS
SIANA
LINDOS
MONOLITHOS
LARDOS
ASKLEPION
APOLAKIA
YANNATHI
KATAGIA
LAKANIA
PALAIOKASTRO

CITY OF RHODES

MANDRAKI
(SMALL
HARBOUR)
TOWER OF
St. NICHOLAS
TOWER OF
NAILLAC
ARSENAL
GREAT
HARBOUR
TOWER
OF THE
MILLS
COLLACHIO
BORGO
GUIDECCA
WALL OF THE JEWS

OPPOSITE. The late fifteenth-
century town of Rhodes.
Bibliothèque Nationale, MS
Lat. 6067, fol. 37v.

Rhodes. The grand master
gives instructions standing in
the centre of the city.
Normal life goes on around
him but an amazing number
of masses are being said in
the background.
Bibliothèque Nationale, MS
Lat. 6067, fol. 33v.

which entailed the proof of injurious behaviour on the other side
– it was aggressive in practice, as demonstrated by the raids of the
Teutonic Knights into Lithuania, by the caravans, or naval cruises,
of the Hospitallers in the eastern Mediterranean and by their use
of the *corso* or legitimized piracy.

The invasion of Rhodes by a combined force of Hospitallers and
Genoese was launched in June 1306, although conquest of the island
and the rest of the archipelago it dominated took much longer than

OPPOSITE. Rhodes. The grand master oversees the repairing of the fortifications. Caoursin, fol. 9v.

RIGHT. The city of Rhodes. Engraving from Sutherland's *The Knights of Malta*, i (Edinburgh, 1830).

BELOW (clockwise). The Kastellania, the court-house of the knights in Rhodes; the gate of the port; the Street of the Knights; part of the fortifications of the city.

expected; it was completed in 1310 by a small crusade under the command of the master. The occupation of Rhodes influenced the papal decision in 1312 to grant the Hospitallers most of the Templars' estates, although it look them a long time to occupy even a proportion of the properties to which they were entitled: they took over those in France only on the payment of huge indemnities in 1317 and had still not taken full possession of those in England by 1338. The establishment of an administration on Rhodes also saddled them with enormous debts. The central convent was not solvent until the 1330s. Among the costs were those associated with the building of fortifications which by the fifteenth century had made Rhodes one of the most heavily defended places in the world. It became an important commercial centre, although the brothers, true to their religious vocation, isolated themselves from the rest of the town in an area of enclosure known as the *collacchio*.

Amboise Gate on the west side of the old town, with the Palace of the Grand Masters behind.

Rhodes and the Sea

Over the centuries the Hospitallers have proved themselves extra-ordinarily adaptable. After the loss of Acre, during the sojourn of their headquarters on Cyprus from 1291 to 1309, they began to change their field of operations from land to sea. They had had a number of transports before 1291, but it was after that date that the decision to build war galleys was taken at the bidding of the papacy. In spite of all the losses of men and matériel at Acre in 1291, the order had some kind of fleet by 1300 – whether built or hired by it is not known. This was a considerable achievement and it demonstrated how the leadership could respond to new demands made on it. On Rhodes the order's battleground definitely became

A sea-fight against the Turks. Late fifteenth-century illustration of a skirmish at sea, showing an Order galley and knights on the left and Turkish soldiers on the right. The manuscripts names those who took part, including three Englishmen. The Hours of Pierre de Bosredon, Pierpont Morgan Library, New York, MS Glazier 55, fol. 140v.

✠ 95 ✠

the sea. It found itself policing the shipping lanes and opposing the Turkish emirs of the coast of Asia Minor and later the rapid expansion of the Ottoman state. Its galleys prowled the shipping lanes, protecting European merchantmen and contributing to the naval leagues that struggled for mastery with the Turks. One hundred brothers in four galleys under their admiral took part in the crusade which sacked Alexandria in 1365. The Hospitaller fleet was comparatively small, being at the most seven or eight galleys, although three was the more usual number in the Rhodian period, rowed by free Greek inhabitants of the islands, not slaves who were very undependable. The galleys were supplemented from the late fifteenth century by a carrack, later a galleon,

OPPOSITE. The grand carrack, the *Santa Anna*. She carried the brothers to Malta in 1530. Sixteenth-century engraving.

OPPOSITE BOTTOM. The order's navy. Oil painting of the capture of a Turkish tartan off the Cape of Tripoli on the North African coast by order ships, under Commander de Fleurigny on the ship *Santa Maria*.

BELOW. Capture of a Turkish ship off Carthage on the North African coast on 18 April 1710 under Commander de Lango.

and after 1700 by a small squadron of ships of the line. In spite of the marked effect of losses on a fleet of this size – three galleys were taken in 1570, which meant that no more than three could be contributed to the league which fought at Lepanto in the following year – the knights of Malta, as the Hospitallers were now called, kept up aggressive sea-raiding into the seventeenth and eighteenth centuries, for example attacking Modon and Corinth in Greece in 1531 and 1611 respectively and Oran in North Africa in 1749. As late as April 1798, when a Tunisian vessel was captured near Gozo, they had four galleys, two ships-of-the-line and two frigates. Since every brother knight had to to serve three *caravans* – naval expeditions of at least six months – to qualify for a commandery in Europe or a captaincy in the navy, every galley carried twenty to thirty ambitious *caravanisti*, providing invaluable training. Hospitallers even lent their expertise to the English navy, while many of the most famous admirals in early modern Europe – Hocquincourt, Suffren, Tourville, Valbette – had received their

Theatres of war of the
Knights of St John. Showing
the naval activities of the
order against the Turks and
the historical sites of their
military activities in the
eastern Mediterranean.
Engraving by de l'Isle and
Delahaye from Vertot's
*Histoire des Chevaliers
Hospitaliers de St Jean de
Jerusalem* (Paris, 1726).

training in Maltese ships. When the Empress Catherine the Great of Russia wanted to establish a galley fleet in the Baltic, she asked for the assistance of a knight of Malta.

Maritime operations were supplemented by the *Corso*, which resembled licensed piracy with the element of holy war added. Regulated by a special tribunal on Rhodes and later on Malta, piratical operations against the Muslims were financed by the Hospitallers and others, with 10 per cent of the spoil going to the grand master. In 1519 the *Corso* was providing the order with 47,000 ducats a year. It also contributed to the Rhodian economy, although the prisoners taken by it and held on the island enraged the Ottoman government and contributed to its decision to invade in 1522. The *corso* was as important to Malta in the sixteenth and seventeenth centuries, and indigenous Maltese played a full part in

PALUS
MEOTIDES

S A R M A T I E
A S I A T I Q U E

TURQUESTAN

NT EUXIN

Mont Caucase

SCYTHIE ou TARTARIE

Sinope

Trebisonde

GEORGIE

MER

COVARZEM
ou CARIZME

MAVRALNAHAR

PENDERACIE

TURCOMANIE

ARMENIE

CASPIENE

CAPPADOCE

PETITE
ARMENIE

Tauris

COROSAN

Mont Caucase

CILICIE

M E D I E

P
E
R
S
E

Golfe de
Laiazzo

Antioche

Baudat

Mont Taurus

I
N
D
E
S

SYRIE

Damas

Euphrate R.

Tigre R.

Jerusalem

Crac ou la Pierre du Desert

QUERMAN

DESERT

Crac de Mont royal

ARABIE PETRÉE

A R A B I E   D E S E R T E

S
E
I
N

P E R S I Q U E

Medine

A R A B I E

MER DES INDES

Tropique du Cancer

la Meque

A R A B I E   H E U R E U S E

Gravé par Delahaye

The *Corso.* Ships licensed by
the order attacking trading
vessels. Engraving,
seventeenth century.

✠ 99 ✠

it. Maltese corsairs were especially active along the Maghrib coast, with occasional forays into the Atlantic. As late as 1675 there were between twenty and thirty of them operating out of the island The numbers then declined, so that by 1740 there were only between ten and twenty. Thereafter they dwindled almost to none.

The Defence of the East

The Hospitallers on Rhodes were active in crusades and crusade leagues, and in the general defence of the remaining Christian settlements in the eastern Mediterranean region. Their soldiers were called in to protect southern Greece, but an attempt by them to take over the management and defence of one of the last of the crusader states in the region, the principality of Achaea, failed when a crusade organized by their master was destroyed in Albania in 1378. They had taken part in the crusade which had captured Smyrna in 1344; and from 1374 to its loss in 1402 they were solely responsible for its defence. Any success in the war of attrition now being waged in the region was dependent on the support of the popes and western public opinion, and the revenues it would bring; and it was probably therefore for propaganda reasons as much as anything that the Hospitallers began to build a great new hospital on Rhodes in 1440. A recognition of the need for good publicity may have been behind the construction of a major new castle on the mainland of Asia Minor, at Bodrum opposite Cos, soon after the loss of Smyrna in 1402. The castle stood on the site of one of the Seven Wonders of the Ancient World, the Mausoleum at Halikarnassos, which the Hospitallers dismantled and robbed for building materials. It was intended to replace the castle at Smyrna – for the defence of which papal indulgences bringing in substantial sums had been granted in 1390 – and it was given the same dedication

Lindos, Rhodes. One of the three cities of Rhodes in classical Greek times, the acropolis and later Byzantine site was developed by the knights as a major fortification. All the citizens and livestock and goods could be gathered in when the Turks raided the islands, which happened frequently. Lindos also housed the prison of the knights where malefactors and knights who transgressed would be incarcerated.

ABOVE. The New Hospital, Rhodes. The order never forgot that a prime function was the care of the sick and it constructed a hospital wherever it established its headquarters.

ABOVE RIGHT. The great ward of the hospital has a small chapel on the left, and inlets into the wall where patients could use a latrine or keep their belongings.

to St Peter; in 1409 the order was permitted to sell plenary indulgences for its defence. Bodrum was not strategically significant, being built on Islamic territory but in a position that was so far from any mainland centre that it was unlikely to provoke a massive reaction from the Turks. The most striking demonstration of its importance to the order's reputation can be seen today on the face of the English Tower, at the south-eastern corner of the enceinte:

Bodrum. Nineteenth-century lithograph showing how the knights incorporated the classical sculptures from the nearby Mausoleum, one of the Seven Wonders of the Ancient World, into their castle. It has been suggested that they were all burnt to make lime for building Bodrum Castle, but this shows clearly that that was not the case. Many of these were removed by the antiquarian Newton in the nineteenth century and are in the British Museum. One knight, Bembo, was a leading figure in the Italian Renaissance. Engraving.

The castle at Bodrum.

a line of English coats-of-arms in stone, at the centre of which are the royal arms of King Henry IV and six other members of his family, and then a further nineteen shields, no less than seventeen of which were those of knights of the Garter, who must have contributed to the building of the tower.

The Fall of Rhodes

Rhodes was seen by the Muslim powers to be a threat to their interests. It was attacked by the Egyptians in 1440 and 1444. By 1470 the order knew it would have to meet an invasion by the Turks. This came in the summer of 1480, when the Hospitallers' successful defence did wonders for their prestige throughout Europe, an English account of it being in print within two years. They were bound to be attacked again and a Turkish armada of more than 400 ships under the command of the Ottoman sultan, Suleiman I, arrived off the island on 24 June 1522. Part of it sailed on to the mainland to ferry over an army which had marched

Hospitaller ambassadors to the court of the Grand Turk. Bibliothèque Nationale, MS Lat. 6067, fol. 93.

The 1522 Siege of Rhodes. An imaginative engraving made for Grand Master de Rohan (1775–97).

Grand Master de l'Isle Adam. Shown as present at the entry of Christ into Jerusalem in this manuscript. British Library, MS Add. 18143, fol. 3v.

OPPOSITE. The Siege of Rhodes, 1480. Bibliothèque Nationale, MS Lat. 6067, fol. 79v.

across Anatolia. By 28 July the whole force was in place, together with its heavy artillery. In 1480 the main attack had come from the sea. Now the Turks launched a series of murderous assaults on the landward side of the city, concentrating particularly on the southern sections of the walls entrusted to the langues of England, Aragon, Provence and Italy. By 4 September much of the bulwark of England had been undermined and destroyed, but the Turks were beaten back by a counter-attack led by Grand Master Philip de l'Isle Adam himself. On the 9th and the 13th the Turks attacked again, and on the 17th they turned their attention to the post of Italy. This was followed on the 24th by a general assault against the whole southern stretch of the walls, preceded by the explosion of mines. In November they crossed the moats before the posts of Aragon and Italy and breached the inner curtain wall. But they had suffered very heavy losses and the sultan, who feared that assistance from the west might arrive, offered terms, which, although at first indignantly refused, led to negotiations in December, interrupted by a final Turkish assault on the post of Aragon. After months of bombardment, mining and direct attack the walls of the city were no longer tenable, supplies were low, and the Greek inhabitants were getting restive. On 18 December the grand master surrendered and, allowed to leave with honour, sailed from Rhodes on 1 January 1523. For some years the Hospitallers were without a home, although it is indicative of their abiding commitment to nursing that their first act was to build a tented hospital on a southern Italian beach. They were, however, soon negotiating for a new base and, on 23 March 1530, the Emperor Charles V granted them the islands of Malta and Gozo and the North African city of Tripoli (which they lost in 1551).

Suleiman I, the Magnificent, Ottoman sultan 1520–66, the conqueror of Rhodes and besieger of Malta. Sixteenth-century German engraving.

There has been a tendency in recent years to confuse Malta's geopolitical importance to the British Empire, and its relationship to the Suez Canal as a staging post on the route to India, with its older place in the Mediterranean order of things, which has been downplayed. Its position, between Italy and Africa, covering, one might say blocking, the narrowest part of the Mediterranean, has always given it strategic significance. Christians and Muslims had disputed it throughout the middle ages and in the sixteenth century warfare nearby intensified, as two great powers, Spain and the Ottoman Empire, fought for control of North Africa. Following the fall of Granada in 1492, Spain had embarked on a policy of explansion, not only across the Atlantic, but also over the straits of

Gibraltar into Africa, leading to the establishment of beachheads along the North African coast, authorized by the popes and inspired by the ancient idea of reaching the Holy Land that way. Melilla was occupied in 1497, Mers el-Kebir in 1505, Oran in 1509 and the Rock of Algiers, Bougie and Tripoli in 1510. A full-scale Spanish crusade was launched against Tunis in 1535. The grim struggle for North Africa lasted for most of the century, only ending with the defeat of the Spanish and the Portuguese and the triumph of the Ottomans in the 1570s.

Malta and Gozo. Hand-coloured engraving by Johann Baptist Homann, Nuremburg, 1702–24.

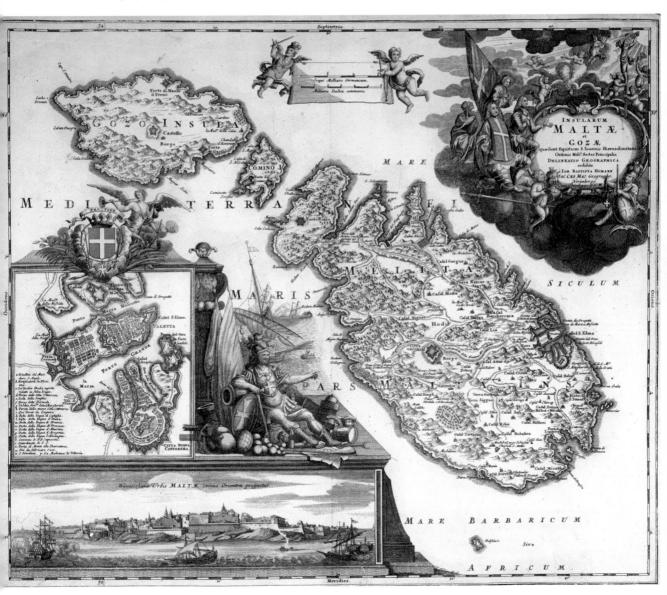

Malta threatened the lines of communication between Istanbul (Constantinople), the capital of the Ottoman Empire, and North Africa: its rulers could disrupt Mediterranean traffic from Alexandria to Algiers. As far as the Emperor Charles V was concerned, as ruler of Spain, it constituted the kind of front line of defence which for centuries had been entrusted by the Castilian kings to the Spanish military orders. With the order of St John looking for a home after the loss of Rhodes, it made sense for it to take up such a position.

Malta and the Great Siege

The surrender of Tripoli, inadequately defended, to the Turks in 1551 was not a heroic episode, but the order soon recovered its reputation. On 19 May 1565 a Turkish invasion force of 25,000 men landed on Malta. To resist them the grand master, Jean de la Valette, had only between 8000 and 9000 men, including around

BELOW AND OPPOSITE. The Great Siege of Malta, 1565. The order's pride in its heroic defence against the Turks was expressed in frescoes in the grand master's palace in Valletta, painted by Matteo Perez d'Aleccio, one-time pupil of Michelangelo. The arrival of the Turks (*below*); the attack on St Elmo (*right*); the 'Little Relief' (*below right*), the arrival of a small body of reinforcements – forty-two brother knights, twenty 'gentlemen' volunteers, including two from England, fifty-six trained gunners and 600 Spanish infantry, which arrived in late June.

LA SMONTATA DELL'ARMATA A MARSASCIROCCO, E CO MERI CONOSCE LE FORTEZZE DI BORGO, E ISOLA ADI 20 MAGG 1565

DIMOSTRAZIONE DI TUTTE LE BATTERIE

IL SOCCORSO PICCOLO AL BORGO DI NOTE TE TEMPO, A DI 3, LUGLIO 1565.

500 brother knights and some brother sergeants-at-arms, 4000 arquebusiers and between 3000 and 4000 Maltese irregulars. The first Turkish attacks were directed against the settlements on the southern shore of the Grand Harbour, Senglea and Birgu (Vittoriosa), which had not been heavily fortified; indeed the knights had strengthened only the sea-castle of St Angelo, the new town of Senglea nearby and, across the Grand Harbour and at its mouth, the fort of St Elmo. On the 24 May the Turks decided to concentrate their forces on the Sciberras peninsula, on the other side of the grand harbour, at the end of which was St Elmo. This small star-shaped fort, a barely recognizable pile of rubble after being under continuous attack for thirty-one days, did not fall until 23 June. Its heroic defence cost the Turks 8000 men and the defenders 1500, including 120 brothers; only nine knights survived to be taken prisoner and they were never heard of again. The long resistance

Portrait medal of Grand Master Jean de Valette. One of many produced, some with different portraits, with the reverse showing symbols of the successful defence of Malta in 1565 and an outline of Valette's planned new city. Italian, 1566.

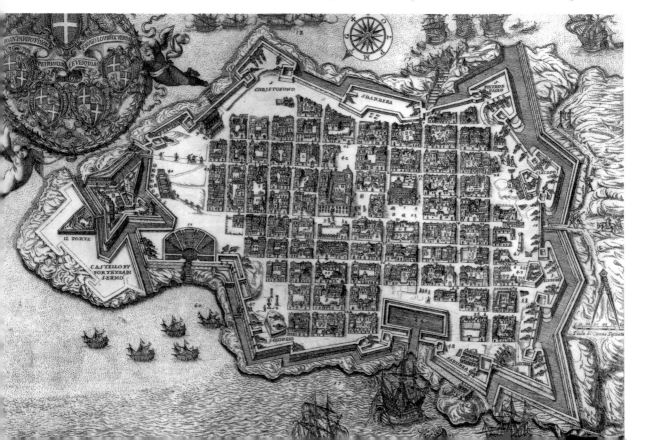

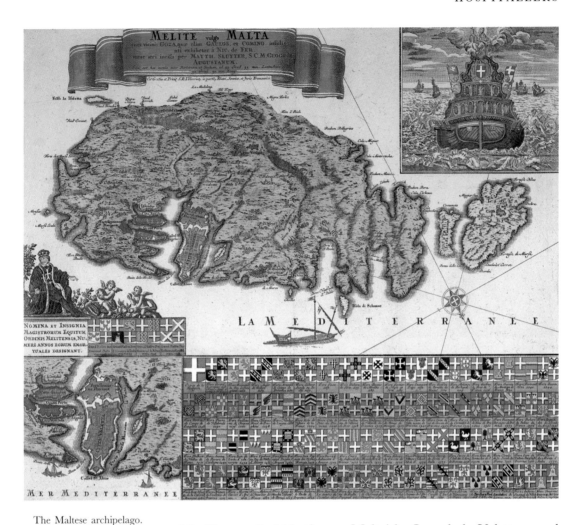

The Maltese archipelago. Malta, Comino and Gozo, with insets of Valletta and the Three Cities, across the Grand Harbour from Valletta, an order ship, the grand master and a large panel containing the coats-of-arms of the grand masters, from 1118 supposedly. The map dates from *c.* 1722–36, but has been re-engraved to add the arms of later grand masters. Hand-coloured engraving by Seutter, after de Fer, Augsburg, *c.* 1730.

of St Elmo, called 'the key to Malta' by Jean de la Valette, saved the island, but that cannot have been clear to the defenders at the time, because the Turks now transported shipping into the Grand Harbour, placed batteries on the Sciberras peninsula opposite the settlements and began to attack them from all sides. The assaults, which were clumsily directed, lasted until 8 September when, having sustained very heavy losses, the Turks withdrew in the face of a relief force of 12,000 Spaniards and Italians brilliantly led by García de Toledo, the Spanish viceroy at Palermo and himself a commander of the order of Santiago. In the midst of the devastation on the shores of the Grand Harbour there stood only 600 of the defenders still capable of bearing arms. Of the 500 brother knights at the start of the siege, 300 were dead and most of the rest were wounded.

The order had been reluctant to take over the Maltese archipelago in 1530. It was homesick for its old headquarters. Its first buildings contain strong Rhodian elements and the early churches it constructed – St John, St Catherine, Our Lady of Victory – were given the same patrons as churches on Rhodes. When thirty-five years later it had to face the Turkish invasion, it did so with

The Three Cities and the Cotonera Lines, Malta. Successive grand masters in Malta continued to fortify the island, right up to the its loss in 1798. In the middle of this painting is Fort St Angelo, with Vittoriosa behind it, and the towns of Cospicua (or Burmola) and Senglea, with Fort St Michael at the end of the peninsula on the right. The inner fortifications, the Sta Margherita Lines, begun in 1639, were later enclosed by the Cotonera Lines, begun in 1670 by Grand Master Niccolò Cotoner. Oil painting, anonymous, *c.* 1671.

minimal defences. Although no invasion recurred, and there was only one later serious Turkish raid on Malta (in 1614), fear of a repeat led to the construction, on the site of the fiercest fighting of Valletta, of perhaps the greatest surviving planned Renaissance city, designed by the Italian Francesco Laparelli and beautified by the great Maltese architect Gerolamo Cassar. Now there could be no turning back and the order's commitment to its Maltese head-quarters was marked in the seventeenth century by the transfer to Valletta of its earliest archives, including the deeds to its claims in and around Jerusalem (should that city ever be retaken), which had been stored in Provence since the loss of the Palestinian coast over three centuries before.

In Valletta the sober magnificence of the churches, auberges and palaces seems to echo the message of the Cyclopean fortifications, the result of an obsessive building campaign, the last element of which, Fort Tigné, was finished only four years before Malta fell to Napoleon in 1798. The brother knights of Malta remained a foreign elite, a closed oligarchic caste which became more and more gerontocratic, refusing to admit into their higher ranks even the Maltese nobles, whose sons could only enter as chaplains, although some families did sometimes arrange for a child to be born in Sicily in the hope of his qualifying for admission. In only one respect were the knights less isolated than they had been on Rhodes. When they built Valletta they did not construct compound

in which they themselves would be enclosed, but scattered their auberges throughout the city. Now that the auberges were fully developed, they themselves were enclosures, although one effect was to make the whole town a kind of ecclesiastical citadel.

The rule of the knights brought to Malta a prosperity reflected in the large parish churches to be found throughout the islands and described in travellers' accounts, which compared conditions very favourably with those on Sicily. The magnificent port facilities around Valletta, and the security the fortifications gave them, led to Malta becoming an important commercial centre, handling a growing volume of shipping and acting as an entrepôt for oriental goods on their way to destinations as distant as the Americas, where the knights themselves had been active in colonial ventures; the United States opened a consulate. The dockyards and arsenals, and the quarantine service, which was internationally regarded as the most efficient in the Mediterranean, provided employment. After 1566, when the decision to found Valletta was taken, the building campaign attracted labourers from the countryside and about 8000 workers from Sicily. The urban complex around the Grand Harbour grew rapidly. By 1590 there were 7750 residents in Valletta

Valletta and the Three Cities, Malta. Valletta, with Fort St Elmo is on the right and to the left, across the Grand Harbour are the Three Cities. To the right in the background is Mdina, the original capital of Malta before the knights' arrival. All sorts of naval activity are shown going on in the harbour. Oil painting, *c.* 1740.

Valletta, showing
fortifications on the Grand
Harbour side. Looking
inland, this shows the marina
and the St Barbara bastion.
Aquatint by Smart and
Sutherland from a painting
by Augustus Earle, 1816.

View of the Three Cities and
the Grand Harbour. Oil
painting by Gianni, *c.* 1860.

and the Three Cities, by 1614 about 11,000 and by 1632 about
18,500. The population of Malta and Gozo rose from 20,000 in
1530 to 50,000 in 1680 and to 90,000 in 1788. This was assisted by
what can only be termed a relatively benevolent, if distant and
rather unimaginative, despotism. The grand masters not only built
Valletta. They also constructed hospitals, especially their main one,
the Sacred Infirmary. They ran a kind of health service for the
population. In 1676 they founded a school of anatomy and surgery
annexed to the infirmary, which became famous, its most outstanding product being Michelangelo Grima, the pioneer of
abdominal surgery. In 1769 they established a university. Discontent

about their rule nevertheless increased in the later eighteenth century, fanned by their often arrogant and discourteous behaviour towards their subjects; it led to a short-lived rising against them in Valletta in 1776.

Malta enabled the knights to survive. Of the plethora of military orders to be found in the early fourteenth century, some, like the English order of St Thomas of Acre, dwindled away; others, like the order of the Temple, were suppressed; most, like the Spanish and Portuguese orders, were secularized and became orders of chivalry. Although its brotherhood is now made up entirely priests, the Teutonic Order survived into the twentieth century by accommodating itself to Habsburg interests, providing a regiment for the Austrian army. Only the order of St John of Jerusalem

Portrait medal of Grand Master Niccolò Cotoner, *c.* 1670.

Portrait medal of Grand Master Menoel de Vilhena, *c.* 1725.

The lapidary floor of St John's church, Valletta. The church floor is paved with nearly 400 memorial tablets in mosaic, commemorating brother knights and adorned with coats of arms, military and naval trophies, and symbols of every kind. It comprises a mausoleum to chivalry. Water-colour, *c.* 1831.

Group of Hospitallers with
the Grand Master.
Right to left: 1. Chaplain;
2. Professed knight with
maniple; 3. Senior chaplain;
4. Grand master;
5. Page to the grand master;
6. Knight. 7. Chaplain.
Oil painting after Favray,
c. 1780.

remains more or less as it was. This is partly because it proved itself to be remarkably adaptable, but it is also because Malta provided it with a role that was considered to be useful, as a defender of Christendom in a continuing holy war which only petered out in the eighteenth century. It is hard to exaggerate the prestige the knights enjoyed in Europe, a prestige reflected in recruitment, because the number of brothers overall rose from 1715 in 1635 to 2240 in 1740. The lifting of the siege of 1565 was celebrated even in Protestant England. It is hardly surprising that the loss of Malta to Napoleon in 1798 shook the order to its foundations. Its somewhat hysterical reaction to the loss of its naval role demonstrates how important that still was to its image of itself.

Malta provided the order with a relatively isolated, self-contained and easily controllable environment, in which its devotional side could be enhanced. Any visitors entering the knights' main church – now the co-cathedral of St John – will be struck by the fact that they have come upon a mausoleum of chivalry, as they are confronted by a floor covered with heraldic devices in multi-coloured

Group of officers of the
order. Oil painting after
Favray, *c.* 1780.

The National Malta Library.
In 1555 the order established
a library, but huge bequests
in 1760 and 1763 meant that
a new one had to be
planned, which, it was
decreed, should also be open
to the public. The building
was completed in 1796, just
before Napoleon's invasion,
and was not, in fact,
inaugurated until after the
knights had departed. It
contains not only the order's
library but also its archives,
with charters going back to
twelfth-century Palestine.
Water-colour by
C. Brocktorff, *c.* 1830.

Déodat de Dolomieu. Born in 1750, he became a member of the order in 1766, but was not a very religious one: it has been said that his chief interests were Malta, science, friendship and love. A great geologist, after whom the Dolomites are named, his career in the order effectively ended with the confiscation of the French commanderies in 1792. He became a professor at the School of Mines in Paris and accompanied Napoleon to Egypt. On the way he helped arrange the surrender of Malta to Napoleon. Engraving by A. de St Aubin, c. 1801.

marble, the memorial tablets of individual knights. They will also gain an impression of a chivalry that was deeply pious. Too much is often made of the lurid escapades in which some young knights got involved. Malta must have been boring for some of them precisely because their elders insisted on behaviour appropriate to the religious life. The early modern nobility, moreover, were sometimes very well educated and the knights' magnificent library in Valletta still testifies to the cultured interests of many brothers, who included men like the archaeologist Louis de Boisgelin and the scientist Déodat de Dolomieu. Others collaborated with reforming bishops and with orders like the Society of Jesus. There was a vestigial strength which enabled the order to reorganize itself in the middle of the nineteenth century, abandon its military role and devote itself to nursing and other charitable activities.

Sovereignty

Malta also gave the order sovereignty. At first, as on Rhodes, the order was not sovereign. It was not entirely clear to whom Rhodes had belonged – the Byzantine emperors or their Latin counterparts – but the order had held it as a fief of the popes. Malta was unambiguously subject to the crown of Sicily and the order held it as a vassal of the king of Sicily, who at the time of its gift to the order was the Emperor Charles V. The grand master had no formal attribute even of semi-sovereignty until 1607, when he was made a prince of the empire, four centuries after a similar title had been granted to the master of the Teutonic Order. Nevertheless, on both Rhodes and Malta, the order behaved as though it was an independent power, minting its own coinage and sending ambassadors to foreign courts, including those of the papacy, France, Spain and Austria. Its de facto status enabled an autocratic Portuguese, Manoel Pinto de Fonseca, who was received as a brother at the age of two and died aged ninety-two after a rule of

Coins of the Order.

Top row, left to right: Gigliato of Roger des Pins (1355–65), showing the master kneeling before the patriarchal cross, and a pine-cone from his arms, to the right. Sequin of Grand Master Pierre d'Aubusson (1476–1503), showing him kneeling before St John the Baptist, the order's patron saint, with the order's banner (modelled on Venetian coinage). Crown of Grand Master Fabrice del Caretto (1513–21), showing St John the Baptist holding the Lamb (symbolising Christ). Tari of Juan de Homedes (1536–53), with the Lamb and Flag (Christ holding the banner of the order).

Second row: 4 tari of Grand Master Jean de la Valette (1557–68) with the order's religious symbol and badge, the eight-pointed cross, later known as the Maltese cross. 4 tari of Valette, showing clasped hands – the building of the new city of Valletta was very expensive and funds ran short, so a copper coinage with the denominations of the real silver coins was issued – these copper coins could be cashed in on leaving the island – the clasped hands and the legend *non aes sed fides* (not bronze but faith) showed that this was all a question of trust. 4 tari of Valette, with the head of St John the Baptist. 4 tari of Valette, with St John the Baptist and the Lamb of Christ.

Third row: Coin of Raphael Cotoner (1660–63). 4 sequin of Ramon Perellos (1697–1720). Sequin of Emmanuel de Pinto (1741–73).

Fourth row: 10 sequin of Antonio de Vilhena (1722–36), designed by the Roman sculptor Soldani. Sequin of Emmanuel de Rohan (1775–97). 30 tari piece of Ferdinand de Hompesch (1797–98).

The grand master as sovereign. Grand Master Emmanuel Pinto da Fonseca after he had assumed sovereignty, painted with his hand resting on the closed crown of full kingship. Oil painting after Favray.

thirty-two years as grand master, simply to assume the closed crown of full sovereignty, even when challenged by the king of the Two Sicilies, and to get away with it. To this day the order remains a 'sovereign entity' recognized by many states.

The history of Malta in the sixteenth, seventeenth and eighteenth centuries is important and unusual, and it is not surprising that an increasing number of historians are engaging in research on it and on the order which ruled it. What are we to make of this order state? One is tempted to treat it as a strange mutation of early colonialism, since here was a foreign, self-contained elite ruling an indigenous population which, although some of its medieval instruments of self-government – in particular the *università* or commune – were still in place, had seen important jurisdictional and administrative functions transferred to new machinery under the order's control. If so, Malta was a strange form of colony, one of a group of eccentric examples of intra-European colonialism – Venetian Crete and Genoese Chios were others – but unlike them governed by rulers who were not economically exploitative: on the contrary, money poured into the island from priories on the European mainland.

If such a point of view had been put to the knights they would never have comprehended it. They would have looked on Malta in the same light, say, as some Italian or German principality, where a foreign ruler could equally have been found lording it over an indigenous population; or they might have compared it to the papal enclave at Avignon, which like Malta was torn from the hands of its occupier in the wake of the French Revolution. They would have considered their government of the island to be a heavy responsibility, the maintenance of an important link in a chain of fortified outposts defending Christian Europe against the world beyond. It is almost certain that had they not been given the island it would have been lost to the Turks, an outcome that would have been potentially as dangerous to the west as the brief Turkish

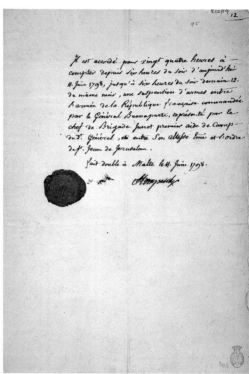

occupation of Otranto in Italy had been in the late fifteenth century. There would certainly have been a reaction and Malta would have become a battleground for far longer than than the few months of the siege in 1565.

The Loss of Malta

The order's ability to defend itself was destroyed by the French Revolution and the revolutionary wars that followed: its revenues fell by two-thirds. All its property in France was seized in 1792 and by 1797 it had lost all its estates west of the Rhine, in Switzerland and in northern Italy. The new grand master, Ferdinand von Hompesch, made approaches to Austria and Russia, which alarmed the French. In June 1798 Napoleon, who wanted to occupy Malta for commercial and strategic reasons, brought his fleet into Maltese waters on his way to Egypt and demanded admission to the Grand Harbour. When the knights tried to stand on their rights as neutrals, he attacked. Of the 332 knights on the island, fifty were too old or ill to fight, and although 200 were French, most of whom were of the ancien régime and bitterly opposed to Napoleon, com-

Grand Master Ferdinand von Hompesch, the last Hospitaller ruler of Malta, who was expelled by Napoleon and deposed by a section of the knights in favour of Tsar Paul I. He spent his last days in lonely exile in Trieste. Oil painting.

The letter of surrender of von Hompesch. Manuscript.

The surrender of Malta. Napoleon lands on Malta, 13 June 1798. In his memoirs he characteristically wrote: '[Malta] certainly possessed immense physicial means of resistance, but no moral strength whatever'. In the six days he spent on the island he established a commission of government and ordered the expulsion of all foreign priests, a reduction in the number of of indigenous priests and religious houses, the abolition of clerical immunity, the liberation of all slaves, the abolition of all titles, the defacement of armorial bearings, the wearing of the French cockade by all Maltese, and the confiscation of all the order's gold and silver.

mand was in the hands of brothers chosen for seniority rather than merit. The ancient guns had not been fired in anger for a century. Powder was found to be rotten and shot defective. The Maltese urban militia was inexperienced and undisciplined. Obsolete plans were put in train. In two days and with hardly any bloodshed the garrison, which was scattered throughout the island rather than concentrated in Valletta, had been overcome. The grand master and his knights were ignominiously expelled.

5

Modern Times

The extraordinary sequence of events which followed the fall of Malta to Napoleon was an unlooked for consequence of one of the most extended legal battles of early modern history. In 1609 Prince Janus of Ostrog made a will leaving his great estates in Poland first to his male heirs, then to the heirs of his brother-in-law and then, if both lines failed, to the order of Malta. In 1672 the order did indeed inherit the lands, but the knight appointed to manage them had obtained a dispensation to marry and on his death his widow enjoyed them herself until 1701, after which a man claiming to be the sole survivor of the family of Janus's brother-in-law took them over with the king of Poland's tacit support. The Ostrog case dragged on until 1776, when the order prevailed and a Polish priory of six commanderies was established. The case had been resolved only because the order had appealed directly to Poland's neighbours, Prussia and Russia, to intervene on its behalf. The appeal to Prussia had entailed the recognition of the Protestant bailiwick of Brandenburg, the Herrenmeister at the time being King Frederick III's brother. The appeal to Russia was to lead eventually to the bizarre mastership of Tsar Paul I.

The priory of Poland was, in fact, a failure. It caused endless worry and provided little in terms of financial support, being disrupted by the Third Partition of Poland in 1793; the Ostrog estates were in one of the regions taken over by the Russians. When Paul I, a romantic who was attracted by the order's history, ascended the Russian throne in 1795 he revived and re-endowed the Polish priory under the title of grand priory of Russia. Then, in the disillusion and anarchy that followed Napoleon's seizure of Malta, the knights of that priory unilaterally deposed Grand Master Hompesch and turned to the tsar. Hompesch, in exile in Trieste, had little support; even the pope had no wish to alienate Russia. On 7 November 1798 the knights in St Petersburg elected as grand master

Tsar Paul I of Russia, wearing the insignia as grand master, which he remained until his assassination in March 1801. A romantic, he dreamed of reviving and extending the order, building in St Petersburg a centre for his Russian Orthodox priory which remained until 1917 the headquarters of the imperial *corps des pages*. Oil painting, 1799.

Paul, who was neither Catholic, celibate, professed nor recognized by the Holy See. Paul ran the order by means of a sacred council composed mostly of non-Catholic laymen and he founded, alongside the Catholic grand priory, a second, Orthodox, grand priory of Russia, using as a precedent the existence of the bailiwick of Brandenburg.

Paul was assassinated on the night of 23 March 1801. His successor, Alexander I, laid no claim to the mastership and urged the legitimate election of a new grand master. After the names of Catholic and professed candidates had been submitted by all the priories, the pope chose Bailiff Tommasi, whose election was ratified by a general assembly of brothers. The council in St Petersburg then voted its own dissolution and surrendered most of the regalia and archives. Tommasi and his successor, the Lieutenant Grand Master Guevara-Suardo, were recognized by the Russians, but Tsar Alexander began to press for the abolition of the Russian priory and in 1810–11 this was brought about by the confiscation of its properties. The abortive grand priory of Russia has, however, continued to haunt the world of orders of St John, because there are now nearly twenty unrecognized orders of St John claiming descent from it.

The Sovereign Military Order of Malta

The events just described demonstrate how far the order, demoralized and near to disintegration, had fallen into chaos in the early nineteenth century. Between 1805 and 1810 the commanderies of Germany and Italy were swept away. The French langues were restored after 1815, but acted independently of the centre. The Spaniards were out of control. The Austrian government had its eye on the priory of Bohemia. The order's headquarters was bankrupt. It is extraordinary that it survived at all, but the appointment of a new lieutenant grand master, Carlo Candida, who was the only surviving knight to have held naval office in Malta, the establishment of its headquarters in Rome in 1834 and the support of Pope Gregory XVI led in the middle years of the nineteenth century to a renaissance and to the emergence of one of the most

S.Gio.di Malta detto il Priorato
13. G.Cassini inc.

remarkable governments, under Candida and his successor Filippo Colloredo, the order had ever had. In an extraordinarily short time the military role it had followed for seven centuries was renounced and the care of the sick was readopted as its prime activity. The provincial structure, shattered by the French Revolution, by the attempts by European states to take the order over and by the growing importance of a class of tertiary knights – of Honour and Devotion – was rebuilt on a new basis, that of national associations. The claims to sovereignty were preserved. The Sovereign Military and Hospitaller Order of St John of Jerusalem, called of Rhodes, called of Malta (commonly known as the Sovereign Military Order of Malta) shares with the Teutonic Order the distinction of having survived as a religious order, owing this to the flexibility with which it has reacted to changing circumstances.

Today the order, although still relatively small in comparison with its medieval past – there are about forty fully professed brother knights (known today as knights of justice) – has the support of some 10,000 lay men and women, who are made knights and dames in various categories by the grand master by virtue of his sovereignty. They constitute a unique body, being members at the same

The Priory of Malta on the Aventine, Rome. This was another Templar property taken over by the the Hospitallers and converted into its priory. Still in the possession of the order of Malta, it has one of the most beautiful gardens in Rome, with a magnificent view across the city to St Peter's. Engraving by G. Cassini, eighteenth century.

time of an order of the church and of an order of chivalry. It is these men and women, grouped in the national associations formed more than a century ago, who engage in much of the charitable work that has brought the order such international prestige in the twentieth century: the projects managed by knights of Malta include a maternity hospital in Bethlehem; hospitals in France, Italy and Latin America; ambulance corps in Austria, Cuba, the Czech Republic, Germany, Hungary, Ireland, Poland and Slovakia; and clinics, orphanages and health centres around the world.

Associated more loosely with it, and mutually recognized by a common declaration of 1987, are the four non-Catholic orders of St John, joined together in an Alliance, which are for obvious reasons not orders of the church, but are Christian lay confraternities and orders of chivalry sharing in the traditions of the order of Malta and legitimized by the recognition of competent authorities, the federal parliament of Germany and the crowns of Sweden, the Netherlands and the United Kingdom.

The Johanniterorden

A province of the medieval order, the bailiwick of Brandenburg, had been formed in the first half of the fourteenth century by the Hospitallers in northern Germany, whose estates had increased with the accretion of Templar properties. These brothers gained the right to elect their own Herrenmeister, subject to the approval of the grand prior of Germany, but at the Reformation many of the commanders in the bailiwick adopted Lutheranism; some married; and the Herrenmeister paid homage to the Protestant duke of Brandenburg. The bailiwick formed part of the complicated confessional pattern of German politics which took a century to settle down; but in the end it bought itself free from the order's headquarters, now on Malta, while remaining in existence as a Lutheran institution. In 1763 it sought partial reintegration into the order with the encouragement of Grand Master Pinto, who wanted the Herrenmeister to use his influence with regard to the Ostrog estates and the re-establishment of the priory of Poland. The bailiwick began to pay dues and even agreed to send deputies to the general chapter of 1776. So in the eighteenth century a non-Catholic 'priory' was being treated by the grand masters as in some sense a limb of the order; while reluctant to recognize it fully, the grand magistracy continued to view the bailiwick in this light, even after it had been suppressed and then re-established by the crown of Prussia in 1852, with the surviving knights of the original foundation.

Die Balley Brandenburg des Ritterlichen Ordens Sankt Johannis vom Spital zu Jerusalem faced disaster in the 1940s. It was persecuted by the Nazis because of its members' adherence to Christian principles and eleven members were executed in the wake of the plot against Hitler in 1944. After 1945 it was deprived of its headquarters and properties in eastern Europe. It now flourishes again. Running hospitals in association with the German government and also working overseas, it has branches in France, Hungary, Austria, Switzerland and Finland. Two other orders have detached themselves from it. In 1920 the Johanniterorden i Sverige was established under the patronage of the king of Sweden; and in 1945 the Johanniter Orde in Nederland formed itself into an independent order with Prince Bernhard, the husband of the queen of the Netherlands, as its head. These two orders are small, but engage in valuable Hospitaller work in their respective countries.

Memorial to the eleven Johanniter Knights executed by the Nazi State.

The British Order of St John

In the confusion that reigned in the early nineteenth century, the French knights of Malta arrogated to themselves the right to manage the order's affairs as a whole through a capitular commission, the authority of which they claimed (through a mistranslation of a papal letter) to have been recognized by the pope. In 1821 power fell into the hands of their chancellor, a man of rash temperament and doubtful origins who called himself the Marquis Pierre-Hippolyte de Sainte-Croix-Molay. With him in charge, the French knights pursued a heady foreign policy with the aim of restoring the order's naval presence in the Mediterranean. The revolt of the Greeks against Ottoman Turkish rule was prospering, attracting romantics and adventurers from all over Europe, and the Turkish empire seemed to be on the verge of collapse. In July 1823 the capitular commission, apparently with the backing of the French government, entered into an alliance with some of the leaders of the Greek revolt, who recognized the order's sovereignty over Rhodes and bound themselves to cede two islands to be stepping stones to its reconquest. In return the order would provide troops and raise ten million francs for the war. Accordingly, an attempt was made in the following November to raise on the London market £640,000 worth of stock, returning 5 per cent, through the issuing of 5000 bonds, redeemable after twenty years.

The treaty was opposed in Greece by rival liberators and the governments of England, Austria and Russia wrecked it. Meanwhile there were rumours that money already raised in London was being misused. In December 1823 the lieutenant grand master published his disavowal of the loan and in 1824 he revoked the capitular commission's powers and dissolved it. The French government, for its part, withdrew its recognition of knighthoods granted by the commission and acknowledged only those specifically authorized by the lieutenant grand master himself. The capitular commission should then have ceased to have any legal existence, but the council of the French langues simply reconstituted itself under the control of Sainte-Croix, confirming the unlimited powers which had already been conferred on him. It still claimed to enjoy the powers of the capitular commission and was as committed as ever to the Mediterranean adventure. In June 1826 it decided to give all Christians, whether Catholic or not, the opportunity to contribute to the recovery of an island headquarters in the Mediterranean and the restoration of the order's ancient naval role. This was a prelude to another appeal to England and two emissaries were authorized to open negotiations with a Scot called Donald Currie, who lived in London.

The agreement made between Currie and the French representatives was recorded in three instruments of convention, which were signed in August 1827. Currie was empowered to raise £240,000 by private subscription. With the money he was to employ men and to buy arms, munitions and vessels for a Mediterranean expedition. The pay and conditions of service of the officers he commissioned were detailed. A 'Gallo-Britannic factory', incorporating a hospital, was to be established to provide a base for merchants in the Levant. Two clauses stipulated that financial subscribers could become members of the order and that all officers commissioned by Currie would also have the right to join it. The instruments were followed by a letter of instruction to Currie, empowering him to set up a hospital to be served by brothers of the Anglican rite, although receptions into the order must accord with its statutes.

While Currie did not raise much money, he recruited a number of Hospitallers, who formed the basis of the new langue. In spite of several attempts, including one that nearly succeeded in 1858,

Florence Nightingale, by Sir George Scharf, 1857. The founder of modern nursing, she was made a Lady of Grace of the Order of St John in 1901.

this nascent English order of St John, which had both Anglican and Catholic members, was never recognized by the grand magistry in Rome as an integral part of the order of Malta. Although the English knights thought up some extraordinary schemes, their visions never materialized and they did virtually nothing charitable: one of them commented in the 1840s that 'as to merit, twenty-three years had passed without the Langue having done anything memorable in that respect'. Instead they dreamed. They were products of a romantic society obsessed by the middle ages and the virtues, as they saw them, of chivalry. Their minds were awash with the glories of the ancient nobility and gentry. They used to sail to dine at Richmond, Kew or Greenwich in pleasure boats flying St John flags. In the late 1830s two of them dressed themselves in dark green coats lined with white and adorned with gilt buttons bearing Maltese crosses, military hats decorated with black feathers, and swords. They recognized all the virtues they most cared about in the order of Malta, of which in spite of everything they believed themselves to be members: the name of the reigning lieutenant grand master in Italy was always placed at the head of their printed material. One of them, Sir William Hillary, who had visited Malta in 1797 and seen Grand Master Hompesch's court in its last days of faded splendour, had raised his own regiment in the Napoleonic War and founded the Royal National Lifeboat Institution – in his old age he continued to play an active and heroic part in sea rescues off the Isle of Man – was typical in this respect. Much of his correspondence was taken up with a plan for the Christian reoccupation of the Holy Land, which would be governed by the order of Malta. He was obsessed with its 'sovereign independence', which he believed to be a safeguard against the political chicanery and jobbery associated with state decorations and as a bulwark against new and unattractive 'democratic' forces.

It was only in the 1860s that the English, under the duke of Manchester (prior, 1861–88), Sir Edmund Lechmere (secretary-general, 1868–90) and Sir John Furley, turned to the work that truly gave them a place in the country's life and rewarded them with royal recognition.

Sir Richard Broun, who was made a knight of St John in 1835 and as registrar and then grand secretary ran the English order from 1837 to his death in December 1858. He made enormous personal sacrifices for the order, but he was an eccentric individual, 'busily engaged in a number of schemes, most of them of a somewhat fantastic nature', which led him once into bankruptcy: he died in great distress. He was obsessed with the extraordinary rights which he believed belonged to the heirs of baronets like himself and he was satirized by Disraeli in *Sybil* as 'Sir Vavasour Firebrace'.

Lady Brassey. Anna Brassey toured the world on her husband's yacht, the *Sunbeam*. Everywhere they went she set up St John Ambulance Association classes and encouraged the spread of ambulance and First Aid work.

The duke of Manchester. The nascent British order of St John developed under his leadership. His royal links helped the British organisation to gain credibility and its philanthropic work to be recognised.

Sir William Hillary, a leading figure in the early years of the English order, had visited Malta in 1797, when he had been the duke of Sussex's equerry, and had seen Grand Master Hompesch's court in its last days.

RIGHT. Sir John Furley. One of the members who attended the Geneva Conference of 1864, he realized that the care needed for battlefield casualties, aid and transport, were also needed for accident victims at work and in the street. Like other members, he worked towards the formation of a British Red Cross organization. He was practical and inventive, devising the Furley stretcher, the Ashford litter (called after and made in his home town), hospital trains and hospital ships. He infiltrated the siege of Paris in 1870, disguised as a coachman, to see how casualties were dealt with.

✠ 131 ✠

Early on they had a stroke of luck. The old priory gatehouse in Clerkenwell had survived the dissolution of 1540, although its occupation since then had been humdrum: a coffee-house, a printer's workshop and an inn. In 1874 the order acquired the freehold and was able, therefore, to occupy at least part of the headquarters of the medieval English Hospitallers.

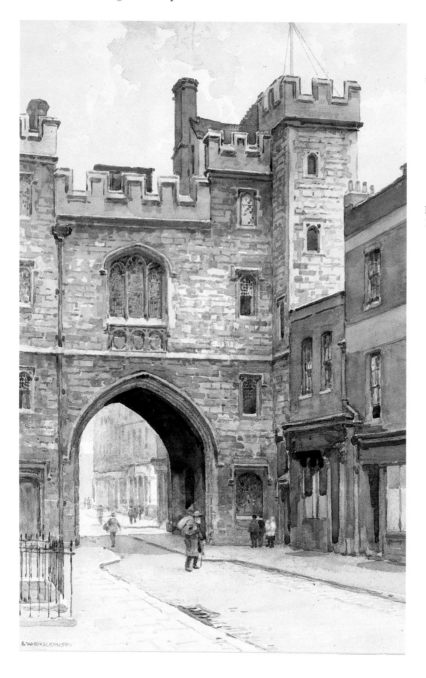

St John's Gate in the nineteenth century. St John's Gate had many roles between the dissolution of the order and its purchase by the British order of St John. The priory was the office of the Master of Revels in Elizabethan times. The gate was home to a coffee-house run by the painter William Hogarth's father, and then the home and printing works of Edward Cave, who gave Dr Johnson his first job when he came to London. Later, it was a public house. Watercolour by E. W. Haslehurst.

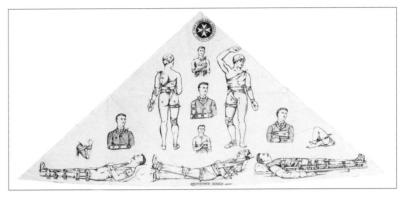

llustrated triangular bandage. Still an important part of first aid equipment, because it is so versatile, the triangular bandage was invented by Professor Esmarch from Germany. The St John Ambulance Association, the training division of the order's Ambulance Department, produced its own supplies.

ILLUSTRATIONS OF THE 'ST JOHN' TWO-WHEELED LITTER.

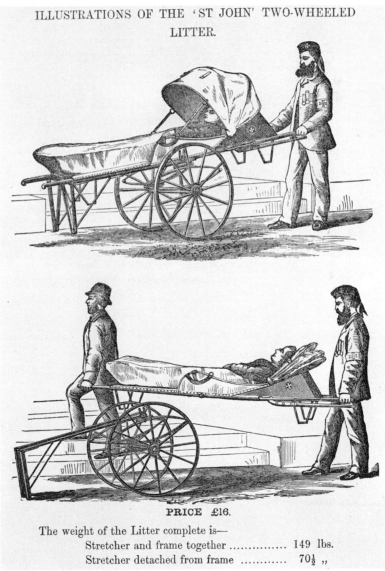

The 'St John' two-wheeled litter. This stretcher was unique, because it could be used to transport patients from the scene of an accident, and transfer them to a train or carriage without disturbing them.

PRICE £16.

The weight of the Litter complete is—
Stretcher and frame together .... 149 lbs.
Stretcher detached from frame .... 70½ „

✠ 133 ✠

The founder of the St John Ambulance Brigade. William Church Brasier, on the horse on the right, was the founder of the first division of the St John Ambulance Brigade at Margate.

There can be little doubt that the direction the English took under the leadership of these remarkable men was influenced by the way the order of Malta was involving itself in the care of the sick in Italy and by the success of the newly founded Red Cross; in 1869 they were represented at an international conference of Red Cross societies held in Berlin. It was clear that while wars were exceptional, injuries were incurred every day in civilian life and that treatment of them would anyway provide training for care in wartime. In 1872 the English were investigating the possibility of establishing an ambulance service in mining and pottery districts, which were the scenes of many accidents, and were considering how to start training courses for those whom we would now call paramedics. The first ambulance service was founded in Staffordshire in 1873. Then in 1874 an 'Ambulance Department' was formed at headquarters. Neither could really develop without volunteers. The breakthrough came after the creation in 1877 of

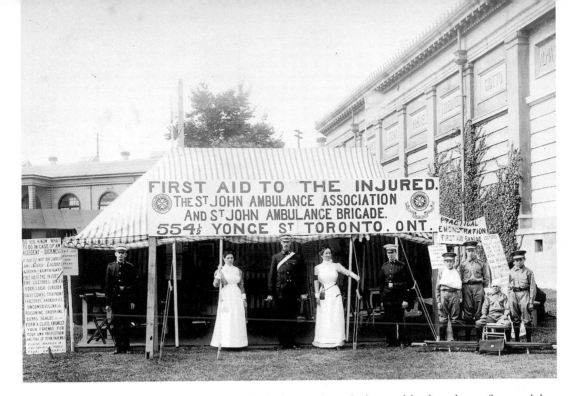

Toronto St John
Ambulance.

A lesson in bandaging. Dock
labourers at Woolwich being
trained in First Aid by Dr
Cruikshank of the St John
Ambulance Association. The
nineteenth-century British
order was so conscious of
working in the tradition of
the Hospitallers that it called
its drive to promote First Aid
up the industrial backbone of
England, 'Ambulance
Crusades'.

the St John Ambulance Association, with the aims of organizing
instruction in first aid and nursing, as well as disseminating 'useful ambulance material', such as bandages, stretchers and litters.
In this field Sir John Furley demonstrated the skill which has given
him the reputation of being one of the great pioneers of the ambulance movement: the Ashford litter, the ambulance hamper,
horse-ambulance carriages and an electric light for searching a
battlefield were all invented or modified by him. Within six months
twelve centres for training in First Aid and depositories for equipment had been established. Six years later others were set up in
Australia, the West Indies, India, Gibraltar and Malta, to be

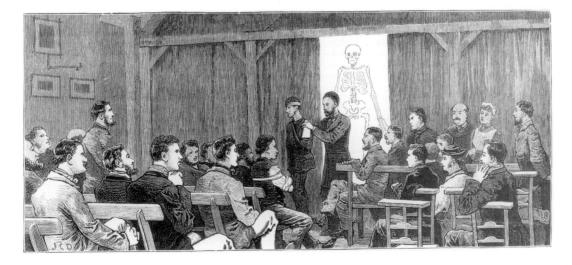

followed by yet more in New Zealand in 1885 and South Africa in 1891, while the idea was copied outside St John's control in Germany, Russia and the United States.

It was now that enthusiastic men and women who had passed the First Aid examination began to form themselves into ambulance and nursing corps, in Kent in 1879 and in Lancashire in 1885. With their number growing rapidly it was decided in 1887 to bring them together into a single body, the St John Ambulance Brigade. By 1902 the number of volunteers had reached 12,000; by 1912 it was 25,000 and by 1921 over 35,000. Growth overseas was even more striking. The first overseas division was established in New Zealand in 1892. Fifty years later the strength of the brigade overseas had risen to 75,000 and by 1965 to 146,000, with representation in almost every part of the Commonwealth.

St John Ambulance, incorporating the association and the brigade, constitutes one of the order's 'foundations'; the other is the Ophthalmic Hospital in Jerusalem. This originated in an

Tibshelf Colliery. The Ambulance Department of the nascent British order of St John had great success in persuading owners of industry to set up First Aid classes and ambulance transport, through the St John organization. Tibshelf Colliery was among the forerunners in 1874.

OPPOSITE. The first St John Ophthalmic Hospital. Oil painting by David Bomberg, commissioned by the warden of the hospital, 1927.

St John Ambulance Brigade Nurses. First Aid and ambulance transport answered some of the health needs of the nineteenth-century community. Another gap was home nursing, at a time when most people were tended at home. St John Ambulance set up nursing divisions. This photograph shows St John Ambulance nurses in the crypt beneath St John's church, Clerkenwell – in the late nineteenth century a very poor district, with many slums, where the nurses dispensed clothes, food and small amounts of money.

RIGHT. The first St John Ambulance nursing divisions were in Oldham and Stoke Newington. Lady Perrott was the first Lady Superintendent.

Queen Victoria. Because of the British organization's pioneering First Aid work and the work of the Ophthalmic Hospital, Queen Victoria granted them a charter of incorporation making them a British Royal Order of Chivalry. The painting shows her holding the charter. Above her, to the left, is a painting of Prince Albert, long dead, wearing his Cross of St John as a member of the Prussian order. Oil painting.

application made in 1876 by Sir Edmund Lechmere to the Ottoman government for the grant of a site in Jerusalem, then ruled by the Turks. A personal approach by the Prince of Wales led to a mandate being issued in 1882. The decision had already been made to concentrate on the treatment of eye diseases and within six months the medical officer reported that 6158 patients had received advice and medicine and 1952 had been treated. Total attendances and operations in 1933 were 89,895 and 3630 respectively and in 1965, before the Israeli occupation of the West Bank, 141,851 and 6089.

The imagination and drive of its leaders in the 1870s and 1880s turned the English from a backward-looking body of dreamers into an energetic modern charitable organization. In 1876 the Princess of Wales accepted membership as a lady of justice. Twelve years later the prince (afterwards King Edward VII), who was already a bailiff grand cross of the order of Malta, petitioned Queen Victoria for a royal charter of incorporation. This charter, which received the royal assent on 14 May 1888, is the basis of the order's status today. St John became an order of the British crown with the queen as its sovereign head and the Prince of Wales as its grand prior. The crown recognized this initiative of the French langues of the order of Malta as having continuity from the medieval Hospitallers: 'The Grand Priory of England is the Head of the Sixth or English Language of the Venerable Order of St John of Jerusalem'.

Wartime

The order was involved in war service as soon as it began to assume an active rôle. On the outbreak of the Franco-Prussian War in 1870 the English knights of St John took the initiative in founding, and in providing several members of, a British National Society for Aid to the Sick and Wounded, which also took measures to alleviate suffering during the Turco-Serbian War of 1876. The growth of the voluntary sector (and the obvious use to which it could be put) induced the Secretary of State for War to convene a conference in 1898. This led to the creation of the Central British Red Cross Committee, consisting of representatives from various bodies, including the St John Ambulance Association. As war in South Africa threatened, a division of responsibilities was agreed. The Central Red Cross committee would coordinate general support for the British army, the St John Ambulance Association would assist in providing comforts and parcels for the troops, and the St John Ambulance Brigade would provide auxiliary orderlies. Within forty-eight hours of the first call for men, St John volunteers were reporting for training and ten days later, on 23 November 1899, the first 'Johnnies' left Clerkenwell to join the hospital ship *Princess of Wales*. In all, 2046 men from St John served in South Africa, a quarter of all the medical orderlies there. Sixty-five of them died, sixty-one on active duty. Two were awarded DCMs for gallantry and eight were mentioned in despatches.

The response was even more impressive during the First World War. Soon after its declaration a joint committee of the Red Cross and the order of St John was formed and the two organizations thereafter worked closely together. The government, which had seen the value of the use of volunteers during the Boer War, encouraged the order to prepare itself for future hostilities. This led to the training of a medical reserve service and the creation of

St John Hospital, Etaples, France. St John members provided medical reserves in the First World War. The Royal Naval Auxiliary Sick Berth Reserve was entirely staffed by St John men, and many were called up to the Royal Army Medical Corps as reserves. St John also ran its own hospitals and provided an entire base hospital at Etaples. Oil painting by E. Miéville, a St John VAD nurse (1917).

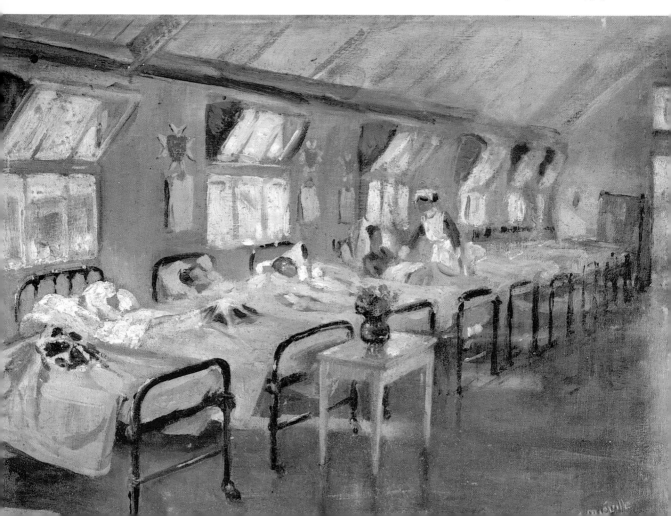

St John VAD Hospital, Rochdale. One of the many St John VAD Hospitals. St John members also staffed Military Home Hospitals, drove ambulances and provided a host of other services, including training the public in First Aid.

complete hospital staffs – the Military Home Hospitals Reserve – to undertake duties in military hospitals at home and a Royal Naval Auxiliary Sick Berth Reserve to serve on hospital ships. Early in August 1914 the RNASBR was mobilized; within thirty-six hours over 850 men had reported to their barracks and within a few weeks some of them were at sea. On 4 August the military hospital reservists were called up; by the 10th all 2000 had reported for duty, and when the War Office called for a further 500 they were immediately found. Soon after the declaration of war trained nurses from the Brigade were providing the complete staff of No. 5 hospital at Wimereux. The most famous of the St John establishments in France was the base hospital at Etaples, with a staff of nineteen officers, seventy-eight nurses and 141 orderlies, which at the end of the war had nearly 750 beds in use. At home the order established, ran and staffed auxiliary hospitals, the largest of which was at Southport; it had 2000 admissions in 1916, including over 750 seriously wounded, and 2500 in 1918. It has been pointed out that it would be hard to find any other organization which could have willingly produced 12,000 trained first aiders and nurses for

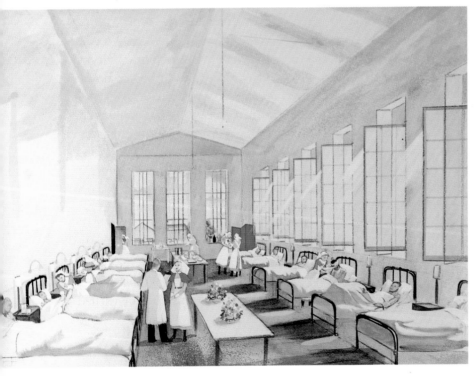

As in the First World War the British Red Cross Society and the Order of St John had a Joint War Organization to coordinate humanitarian services in the Second World War. They provided parcels for prisoners-of-war, a missing persons tracing service, help for refugees, comforts and welfare for troops, and homes for disabled ex-servicemen. These paintings are part of a series of designs for dioramas which toured the country to raise money for the work of the Joint Committee. Doris Zinkeisen, and her sister Anna were official war artists for the Joint Committee. These scenes show the packing of materials for prisoner-of-war parcels, and a hospital staffed by St John and Red Cross nurses. Water-colours by Doris Zinkeisen.

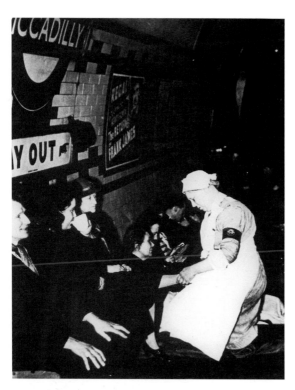

St John members in the Blitz. St John provided many humanitarian services and training for the public in air raid precautions.

active service in the first six months of the war. By the time compulsory conscription was introduced in 1916 over 45,000 men and women had been mobilized.

Cooperation with the Red Cross was maintained in peacetime and the reservists were kept in being. When during the Munich Crisis in 1938 the government asked for the 755 men of the RNASBR to be called up, they reported within two days. In the Far East St John in Hong Kong took charge of a five hundred bed hospital after the Japanese invasion of China in 1932. With the coming of war in 1939 a new Joint War Organization, with a central committee consisting of forty-eight members, twenty-four each from the Red Cross and the order, was able to swing into action as a channel for relief work and medical assistance at home and overseas. St John also carried on with work of its own: instructing the War Reserve Constabulary and the Home Guard in First Aid; engaging in stretcher and ambulance work – the brigade now reached a strength of nearly 200,000 personnel; sending ambulances and their crews to France; and, as in the First World War, serving in the RNASBR and Military Home Hospitals Reserve. By the end of August 1939 1606 St John personnel had reported to the navy and by the end of the year nearly 2500 had reported to the army, while another 2000 men and women were working in hospitals in Britain. St John provided First Aid posts in London tube stations during the Blitz: at the height of the bombing more than 50,000 St John men and women were working in the civil defence systems. Members of the Association and Brigade were even active in prisoner-of-war camps in Germany, volunteering for medical duties and as instructors. In Stalag 383 in Bavaria nearly 300 prisoners successfully sat the examinations in First Aid, nursing and hygiene: by the end of 1944 500 certificates had been awarded and 1500 camp accidents had been dealt with.

The Most Venerable Order of St John Today

The order's status in Britain is unique. It is an order of the British crown, but differs from all others in that. Although all admissions and promotions to the five grades of serving brother or sister, officer, commander, knight or dame (of justice or grace) and bailiff or dame grand cross are approved by the sovereign, and the insignia are worn as official decorations, candidates, who are expected to spend time and effort fulfilling the order's ideals, are put forward by the order itself and once members do not use any title. Most of them have worked for many years in the foundations. In England St John Ambulance has 60,000 members, grouped in

St John Ambulance members in the 1950s. These paintings were used as recruiting posters to try and maintain numbers after the war, when membership dropped. The St John Cadets had been formed in 1922. They rapidly became a popular youth organization, whose members are not only trained in First Aid and Home Nursing but in a range of useful abilities and adventure skills.

Some Acts of Bravery by St John Personnel in War

William Griffin (Wigan) was one of sick-berth staff on HMS *Glendower* off Dunkirk. When another navy vessel, HMS *Snaefell*, signalled for medical help, Griffin was sent over to her in a small boat. Thereafter for two crossings and under continuous enemy gunfire he 'displayed courage and outstanding ability', according to his commanding officer.

James Butler (Worthing) was taking two wounded men to the rear during the North Africa campaign when enemy aircraft machine-gunned his ambulance. Butler was wounded but dragged the two casualties to safety just before the ambulance blew up. He was awarded the Military Medal.

George W. Beeching (Wallasey), who had joined the Brigade as a cadet, was a sick-bay attendant on HMS *Ibis* off Algiers. Ignoring the fact that the ship was sinking, Beeching helped a badly burned man to the deck, gave him his own lifebelt and assisted him gently into the water. As the ship's surgeon later wrote, 'The minutes that Beeching gave to save a shipmate cost him his life'. He received the rare Albert Medal in gold posthumously.

Henry Eric Harden (a sergeant in the Northfleet Division, Kent), a lance-corporal in the RAMC and the orderly attached to a Royal Marine commando troop during the battle of Arnhem, went forward 120 yards under a hail of machine-gun and rifle fire to attend to four casualties left in the open when the section had changed position. After dressing the wounds of three men, Harden carried the fourth back to cover. He was ordered not to go forward again, but all attempts to rescue the remaining three casualties failed. Harden then insisted on venturing out with a stretcher party, but was killed.

> Lance-Corporal Harden displayed ... personal courage of the very highest order, and there is no doubt that it had a most steadying effect upon the other troops in the area at a most critical time. His action was directly responsible for saving the lives of the wounded brought in. His complete contempt for all personal danger, and the magnificent example he set of cool courage and determination to continue with his work, whatever the odds, was an inspiration to his comrades, and will never be forgotten by those who saw it.

Harden was posthumously awarded the Victoria Cross.

3000 divisions in forty-six counties. Over half of them are under the age of eighteen, enrolled in the youth sections as badgers and cadets. St John is the country's leading first-aid training organization, instructing up to half a million people a year in England, Wales and Northern Ireland. Its members treat 200,000 casualties a year. In Jerusalem the original Ophthalmic Hospital, which still stands, was built on the Bethlehem road, not far from the Jaffa Gate and within sight of the ruined twelfth-century Hospitaller cemetery church at Acheldamach. The partition of Palestine left it on the wrong side of the frontier as far as its Arab patients were concerned and in 1948 it moved into the Old City itself, to a house

The St John Ophthalmic Hospital, Jerusalem. The hospital moved into new buildings in 1960 and continues to provide the highest standards of eye care, supported by St John round the world.

Hospital Outreach clinic in Gaza. St John is developing primary health care and early treatment programmes with its Outreach clinics.

in the Muristan, the site of the original twelfth-century hospital. This proved to be too small – in 1959 it was treating 164,000 patients – and a new hospital outside the city on the Nablus road and a little to the north of the Damascus Gate was officially opened in 1960. It is one of the busiest ophthalmic centres in the world. Over 55,000 outpatients are seen each year and of these over 4500 are treated by St John's surgeons. It provides training. It also has a clinic in Gaza and travelling outreach clinics which visit Palestinian villages on the West Bank.

The order has 30,000 members worldwide, while St John Ambulance has over 200,000 volunteers in some forty countries. By 1905 there were already fifty divisions of the St John Ambulance

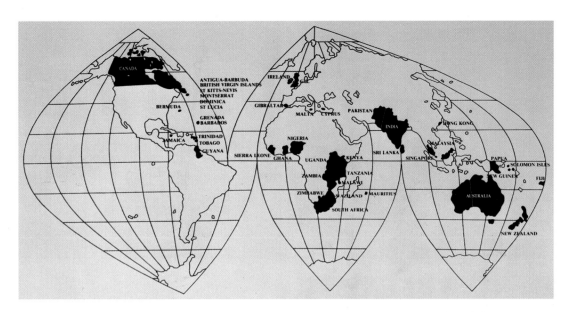

St John Worldwide. The order of St John has establishments in most Commonwealth countries, and St John Ambulance is present in many more around the world, bringing vital First Aid treatment and other training to remote or highly populated areas.

Brigade overseas: twenty-one in New Zealand, fifteen in Australia, eleven in South Africa and three in India; they were to be followed by divisions in Canada, Malta, Ceylon (Sri Lanka), Hong Kong and Gibraltar. It was clear that sooner or later the growth in the empire would demand a measure of decentralization and in 1907 a supplemental royal charter empowered the grand prior to establish subordinate priories overseas, although in the event the only one created was that of Wales, near at hand, in 1918. In 1926, however, a new royal charter not only amended the order's title from 'Grand Priory in England' to 'Grand Priory in the British Realm' – the last four words were dropped in 1974 – and granted the prefix 'Venerable' (expanded to 'Most Venerable' in 1955) to bring the order's title into line with those of other British orders of chivalry, but also laid down a pattern of imperial organization. Commanderies could be established overseas which would, if conditions warranted it, be elevated to the status of priories with commanderies under them. The first commandery, that of Southern Africa, was established in 1927, to be followed by New Zealand in 1931, Canada in 1934 and Australia in 1941. South Africa became a priory in 1942, as did Canada, Australia and New Zealand in 1946, and Scotland in 1947.

It is often hard for members of the public to understand what the order itself does. St John Ambulance is well known, because its uniformed volunteers are in evidence on almost every occasion where large numbers of people gather, but the order behind it is

St John members around the world.

OPPOSITE (*clockwise from top left*). First Badger set in Barbados; Indian St John Ambulance; St John Ambulance, Australia, at the Canberra Show; Canada St John Ski Rescue Team; care in the community in South Africa; Muslim Cadets, Malacca, 1990.

ABOVE. Malawi; Hong Kong.

not often in the news, although it is the governing body, responsible in the last resort for management and finance; if anything went wrong, it would be the order, not the foundations, which would have to shoulder the blame. One of the main functions of all the recognized orders of St John is to preserve and publicize the traditions which make the work of their foundations distinctive.

St John Badgers. The two newest parts of St John are at opposite ends of the age spectrum. The Badgers are aged between six and ten, and learn First Aid and many other skills enjoyably. The St John Fellowship is made up of former St John Ambulance members who meet together socially and continue to help the work of St John by contributing their skills and experience.

St John at work today. St John Ambulance is the country's leader in First Aid training, and its volunteer members continue to provide a First Aid service to the public. They are still seen 'wherever crowds gather' and increasingly are on hand to help to care for their communities.

There are many things about St John's military past which are alien or irrelevant to us today, but they have their use in contributing to discipline, rigorous standards and integrity. On the other hand, in their care of the sick the early Hospitallers foreshadowed in a remarkable way what the modern orders do. They made no distinctions as far as the religion of their patients was concerned. Their great hospitals in Jerusalem and Acre set standards for nursing care which were not to be found again until the nineteenth century. They sent out teams to bring in those who were too ill to admit themselves. Their surgeons served in a mobile tented hospital that accompanied Christian field armies. They had an 'outreach' programme to care for mothers too poor or unwell to look after their babies properly. They ran a major orphanage. Their example provides the modern volunteers with their inspiration and with a model, particularly in the treatment of the poor. The five recognized orders acting together constitute a major international force for good, with approaching half a million volunteers at work throughout the world.

The Future

As its constitution evolved, the Most Venerable Order of the Hospital of St John of Jerusalem naturally reflected the model provided by the empire, including control by a central headquarters which was overwhelmingly English. This made less sense as the imperial territories became independent sovereign countries and the work of St John was taken up in regions outside the Commonwealth, including the United States, where there is now a priory. Since the middle of the 1980s, therefore, the old imperial model has been progressively abandoned. Although most members are admitted to the order with the sanction of Queen Elizabeth II as queen of the United Kingdom, Canadians have been admitted since 1991 with the sanction of the queen as queen of Canada and Australians since 1998 with the sanction of the queen as queen of Australia. The culmination of this process has come in 1999, with the order being reconstituted to give parity to its overseas priories. A priory of England will in future rank equally with them, while the chapter general, largely an English body which up to now has had the last say in the government of the whole order, is being abolished. The order's central government will now be a grand council, whose members will include the prior or chancellor of each priory throughout the world.

From 1999, therefore, the order is being reconstituted to reflect the fact that it is international, while continuing to be an order of chivalry established by the British crown. In reconstructing itself to meet the needs of a post-imperial world it is showing the adaptability which has been the hallmark of St John for nine centuries. That adaptability has always served one purpose, whether narrowly interpreted in some periods as the defence of Christendom or more broadly throughout as the care of the poor and sick of all religions and races: the service of mankind.

Her Majesty the Queen, Sovereign Head of the Order of St John.

Further Reading

The general history of all the military orders in the central middle ages has been covered by A. J. Forey in *The Military Orders from the Twelfth to the Early Fourteenth Centuries* (London, 1992) and is carried further – to the end of the eighteenth century – in chapters written by him and by A. T. Luttrell in J. S. C. Riley-Smith (ed.), *The Oxford Illustrated History of the Crusades* (Oxford, 1995; paperback 1997). A more popular survey is to be found in D. Seward, *The Monks of War: The Military Religious Orders* (2nd edn, London, 1995).

On the order of St John of Jerusalem itself, H. J. A. Sire, *The Knights of Malta* (New Haven and London, 1994) takes the story from its origins to modern times. A planned four-volume academic history never got further than J. S. C. Riley-Smith, *The Knights of St John in Jerusalem and Cyprus, c. 1050–1310* (London, 1967), but the course of academic studies can be traced in the published papers of conferences, especially M. Barber (ed.), *The Military Orders: Fighting for the Faith and Caring for the Sick* (London, 1995) and H. Nicholson (ed.), *The Military Orders*, ii, *Welfare and Warfare* (Aldershot, 1998), and in the collected papers of scholars such as A. J. Forey, *Military Orders and Crusaders* (Aldershot, 1994) and A. T. Luttrell, *The Hospitallers in Cyprus, Rhodes, Greece and the West, 1291–1440* (London, 1978), *Latin Greece, the Hospitallers and the Crusades, 1291–1440* (London, 1982), and *The Hospitallers of Rhodes and their Mediterranean World* (London, 1992). For a possible English master in the thirteenth century, see C. R. J. Humphery-Smith, *Hugh Revel, Master of the Hospital of St John of Jerusalem, 1258–1277* (Chichester, 1994) and for an early summary of the sensational archaeological discoveries in Acre, see A. Kesten, *The Old City of Acre: Re-Examination Report 1993* (Akko, 1993). Dr Luttrell, whose collected papers are referred to above, specializes on the history of the order on Rhodes, for which see also E. Kollias, *The City of Rhodes and the Palace of the Master* (Athens, 1988). For the order on Malta, see R. Cavaliero, *The Last of the Crusaders: The Knights of St John and Malta in the Eighteenth Century* (London, 1960), A. Hoppen, *The Fortification of Malta by the Order of St John, 1530–1798* (Edinburgh, 1979), V. Mallia Milanes (ed.), *Hospitaller Malta, 1530–1798: Studies in Early Modern Malta and the Order of St John of Jerusalem* (Malta, 1993), and H. P. Scicluna, *The Church of St John in Valletta: Its History, Architecture and Monuments, with a Brief History of the Order of St John from its Inception to the Present Day* (San Martin, Malta, 1955). The museum of the order at St John's Gate has published several catalogues of items in its collection devoted to Malta. S. Dyer, *Malta Views: A Catalogue of Topographical Prints and Drawings of Malta in the Museum of the Order of St John* (London, 1984); J. Findlater and P. Willis, *Silver at St John's Gate: Maltese and other Silver in the Collection of the Museum of the Order of St John* (London, 1990); J. Toffolo, *Image of a Knight: Portrait Prints and Drawings of the Knights of St John in the Museum of the Order of St John* (London, 1988).

For further details of the history of the Most Venerable Order it is still worth consulting E. King, *The Knights of St John in the British Realm*, revised and continued by H. Luke (London, 1967). The history of St John Ambulance is covered by R. Cole-Mackintosh, *A Century of Service to Mankind: A History of the St John Ambulance Brigade* (London, 1986) and is illustrated in J. Toffolo, *St John in Focus: A History of St John Ambulance in Photographs from the Museum of the Order of St John* (London, 1987), P. Kernaghan, *St John Ambulance in Victorian Britain* (London, 1994) and P. Kernaghan, *St John Ambulance in World War Two* (London, 1995). A good example of the many publications devoted to St John in the empire and commonwealth is G. W. Rice, *Ambulances and First Aid: St John in Christchurch, 1885–1987: A History of the St John Ambulance Association and Brigade in Christchurch, New Zealand* (Christchurch, 1994). A video-history of the order, *The Story of the Eight-Pointed Cross*, is available from the Order of St John, St John's Gate, Clerkenwell, London ec1m 4da.